Snapshots

Snapshots

✦

Memories of Growing Up on Hopewell Hill

Brian L. Dowler

Writers Club Press
New York Lincoln Shanghai

Snapshots
Memories of Growing Up on Hopewell Hill

All Rights Reserved © 2002 by Brian L. Dowler

Writers Club Press
an imprint of iUniverse, Inc.

For information address:
iUniverse, Inc.
2021 Pine Lake Road, Suite 100
Lincoln, NE 68512
www.iuniverse.com

ISBN: 0-595-25880-8 (pbk)
ISBN: 0-595-65400-2 (cloth)

Printed in the United States of America

First, I would like to thank my parents, who raised me up in a protective and loving environment, where I could enjoy my childhood experiences among the interesting people of Hopewell Hill.

Second, I would like to thank my wife Cathy, and children Ashley, Joshua and Jacob, who endured this project of mine with understanding. I love you all.

"Wish I didn't know now, what I didn't know then…"

—Bob Segar

"The good times weren't always so good, tomorrow ain't as bad as it seems…"

—Billy Joel

Contents

Preface

I grew up in a rural section of Wood County, West Virginia, known as Hopewell Hill. Wood County is on the western side of the state, where the Ohio River forms a wide boundary between West Virginia and the state of Ohio. This part of the West Virginia is not characterized by mountains, but by rolling hills leading into the river flatlands. Hopewell Hill is the highest elevation in Wood County. Lightning, high winds, or hail might hit us, but one thing was for sure; we didn't have to worry about floods. From our vantage point, we lived on top of the world.

Shortly after they were married, my parents, Ernie and Eva Dowler, bought a parcel of land from my aunt and uncle, Averill and Geneva Kaufman. They built a brick ranch house on the crest of this land, providing a forward view over Route 68 and a downward view of farms in the valley. My mother grew up in this valley, where her parents scratched out a farmland living. Like many of the old homesteads in the area, my grandparents' large two-story farmhouse, barns and numerous outbuildings, lapsed further and further into disrepair until they were finally torn down and burned not long ago. The old homesteads were often abandoned by my parent's generation. My parents, who after a tough childhood craved for and could afford more modern conveniences, like flushing toilets and running water, were no exception. In quick succession they started a family—my older sister Leslie was born in 1960, and I followed in 1962. Nine years later, my younger sister Hope was born.

Our house actually sat along the side of a short "loop" of the old Route 2 that was left over when the road was improved. During my childhood, the road had to be renamed, as a new governor was voted into office after promising to upgrade Route 2 as part of his political platform. When he got into office and realized that funds were not available to fulfill his plan, he had Route 2 renamed to Route 68, then made some token improvements to an existing 4-lane road many miles away, which he then had relabeled as Route 2. All we got out of his shifty campaign promise was a new address. We wrote this off to the normal shenanigans of democratic politics, and besides we were secretly relieved that the road remained a two-lane highway.

This is a land of "runs", dirt roads that were first forged in the days of horseback travel, which tend to follow the crests of hills and the creek flatlands. To the left of our house was a graveyard, which separated us from the white country church building belonging to the Hopewell Church of Christ, which we attended faithfully along with most of the people in our immediate neighborhood. On the other side of the church building was Pine Run, which immediately shot downward toward the west from Route 68 and formed the southern side of our property line. My good friend Danny Camp lived at the first house, a quarter-mile or so down the dirt road. Just past Pine Run was the "parsonage", which was built when I was in grade school. This is where the minister Jim Phillips lived, along with his wife Enola and four children, including my best friend Joey. On the right side of our house the Penn's occupied a small white house on a half-acre lot. Much to my chagrin they had four girls, none of whom had any interest in football, hunting, or any other testosterone charged activities. Their house was sandwiched between our property and the large green farmhouse owned by Averill and Geneva. Bloomer's knob, the second highest hill in the county, characterized the other side of Route 68. This was located just past Gunners Run, which ran east from the main road.

Our little patch of houses formed a suburban oasis in the midst of wooded hills and country farms. Here we were sheltered from the turbulence of the 60's and 70's; we forged strong friendships with neighbors, yet we enjoyed the sedate country lifestyle, and witnessed the beauty of God's creation. It was a safe place, quiet and relaxed, where the peaceful sanctity of our home was disturbed only by occasional pleas of help from stranded motorists who broke down along the highway. It was a great place to grow up.

It was in Hopewell that I lived out my childhood, where I wandered the country roads during daylong bicycle trips that were not fearfully discouraged, but confidently encouraged. Our primary dangers within this safe haven were not strangers but ourselves, as we constantly carried slingshots or BB guns, made homemade bombs from gasoline and gunpowder, and fashioned jumps for our bicycles and dirt bikes. The wide-open fields were great for learning to drive, and we all started out on tractors and then moved up to farm trucks. I walked the fringe of these fields in the summertime for miles, picking wild blackberries by the bucketful. We fished the many local ponds with free reign. I can still remember pulling a five-pound largemouth out of the tranquil water, then rushing home to proudly show the monster fish before scaling it on the front porch, to my mother's chagrin. As I grew into manhood, I learned how to set barbed wire fence, cut boards at a sawmill, run a chainsaw, troubleshoot mechanical problems, and dress game.

West Virginians are strong, resolved and moral, made of the tough pioneer stock. Our forefathers tamed the land with backbreaking work, turning rugged woodlands into farmlands that sustained generations. Few full-time farmers remain today. Most men have found more lucrative work in the plastic and chemical factories along the Ohio River. But still the tradition carries on, with many of these men tending small family farms in addition to full-time industrial jobs. The good people of Hopewell Hill are deeply religious, and worship in the conservative traditions of their parents and grandparents. Their love of hunting remains unsurpassed, ingrained into the fiber of generation after generation, and it is still the primary recreational activity of the fall and early winter months.

The places, events, and characters of my childhood slowly forged me into what I am today, leaving an indelible impression. Even though I now live over 300 miles away, I often close my eyes and dream for a moment, and find myself back on Hopewell Hill. I hope you enjoy reading about my childhood as much as I enjoyed living it.

Acknowledgements

A special thank you goes out to my sister Leslie, who provided me with ideas for several of the chapters in this book.

My sincere appreciation goes out to Colleen Glennon, for her invaluable help and support in editing this book.

A big "thank you" goes out to Nita Hammersmith, Steve Cantrell, Jerry & Jeanette Dyer, and all the other people who encouraged me to continue to put these stories on paper.

Finally, I want to thank all of the good people of Hopewell Hill, who taught me the meaning of extended family and showed me how to be a good neighbor.

Field of Champions

It was one of those defining moments in my youth, a moment so magical to me as a young boy that it is forever burned into my memory.

It was the early 1970's; I can't be any more specific than that. The dry heat of summer had firmly grasped the hills of West Virginia. One of the highlights of my boyhood summers, in addition to homemade ice cream, hot dog roasts, and playing softball with the men at church picnics, was helping the farmers to put in their precious crop of summer hay. And when I was 10 or 11, being invited onto the hallowed hay field was akin to a rite of manhood, an opportunity for me to demonstrate that inside the small wiry frame and behind those plastic horn-rimmed glasses was a young man trying to burst his way onto that hallow ground tread only by men.

Every boy should have the opportunity to put in hay. Not the round bales favored by today's sophisticated and part-time farmers, requiring little manual labor, but honest-to-goodness square bales. Forty pounds of scratchy stubble, alfalfa dust, baler twine, and an occasional copperhead snake. As a young boy, I was delegated to ride the wagons and trucks as a "stacker"; I was still too young to loft those bales over my head onto the upper levels of the wagons. But that was ok; I was part of the team, glad to be associated with the older boys, in their faded jeans and sneakers, their shirts off and skin hued to a deep bronze after days and days in the hot summer sun.

One summer day, after loading the barn with hay, it was time to head back out into the field. I was riding shotgun in the old blue Ford with my dad, leaning out of the open window to watch the progress of the other vehicles. As the tires crunched over the freshly mowed stubble, my cousin Dave and his friend pulled up beside of us. Dave was

1

one of the older boys, and had saved up his money to buy a Chevy coupe, which he in turn had souped up and turned a hot rod, at least as much as a country teenager could do. Revving his engine, he pulled along side us, grinned, and challenged my father to duel.

It was a hopeless case—our old Ford pickup against Dave's coupe. We might as well have been lined up next to Mario Andretti or Richard Petty. Never one to turn down a challenge, my dad smiled and punched the accelerator of the old Ford, hoping for a second or two of advantage. The dust flew as the two vehicles strained in the hot summer sun. I waited for the inevitable, knowing in my heart that our was a hopeless cause.

Then the impossible happened; Dave punched his motor too hard, and his mail order Holley 4-barrel choked on too much fuel and died. I can still remember leaning out the window, looking back in disbelief as Dave and his friend ran out and popped the hood, hoping for a quick fix, praying they could repair it fast enough to overtake us to the end of the field. But their engine was completely flooded; we coasted to a remarkable victory. And my dad, who now seemed eight feet tall, grinned as though he knew all along this would happen. We had won an impossible victory, and were for one day, inexplicably, champions of the field.

Today, I find myself in the same situation. I am aligned in a duel with someone more powerful and stronger than I am. To the outsider, it appears that Satan has all the advantages, and there is no way I can win. But as I head for the finish line, I find myself riding shotgun with my heavenly Father. And when I reach the finish line, just like that magical time many years ago, I will look back and see Satan stalled, his hood up, and myself hopelessly out of his reach. And I will revel in the fact that once again, I will have won an impossible victory, and I will join the ranks of champions.

Spot

Spot had been around for as long as I can remember. Which makes sense, because for all I know Spot had been around before I was born. But as I became well entrenched in my early teenage years this faithful hound was approaching the twilight of his life.

Spot maintained a constant presence on our small West Virginia farm. Other dogs came and went, most of them victims to the perils of Route 68, which ran in front of our house. But Spot had two things going for him. First, when it came to the perils of the road, he was darned lucky. More than once he ran across the road with other dogs, only to have one of them meet their maker while he somehow made it out alive every time. I remember my mother, after one such episode, woefully wishing that Spot had been the one to have been hit and killed, not the other dog. After all, Spot was "just" a common farm dog, and although probably a purebred hound, he was no match for our other dogs in the eyes of my mother or sisters. These other dogs were usually collies, German shepherds, or some other mutt mix containing at least some fractional heritage of a "classier" breed of dog.

Second, he was usually home bound, attached to his dog house with a 12 foot piece of chain. He was rather clever though, and had invented a myriad of ways to twist, chew, pull and snag his collar, snap or chain to win temporary bouts of freedom. My dad was constantly on his toes, modifying eyebolts, wiring snaps shut, and fortifying chain links with twisted wire in an effort to limit his escapades.

In his prime, Spot was one of the best rabbit dogs around Hopewell Hill. And though I had only joined in on a few rabbit hunts, I knew this was certainly the best type of hunting to be had. When hunting deer or squirrel, you had to sit still and be quiet, waiting patiently for your prey to come into view, which can be torture to a boy of 13 or 14. But hunting rabbit, that was another story. You can actually walk around, talk, and make all the noise you want, while the dogs skillfully seek out the rabbits and flush them out of the brush piles and thickets. You could always tell when Spot had a rabbit on the run, because his tone changed from a rapid high-pitched bark to a woeful deep baying that echoed across the valleys. I was always amazed at how the dogs, as they ran their tell-tale zigzag pattern through the woods and fields, knew to circle the rabbits back toward you, giving you a chance to line them up in the sights of your Remington 16-gage.

On one occasion, Spot pulled his chain off from the doghouse and ran away in a burst of freedom. Discovering the small length of chain still attached to the doghouse, I only knew that he was out running around, ignorantly dragging a 10-foot section of dog chain. After a day had gone by, I was frantic to find him, sure that the chain was now tangled, and the poor dog was languishing with no food or water in the hot summer sun. But he could have been anywhere within a 1–2 mile radius of the house, and finding him would be nearly impossible. Using my instincts, I headed northwest, through Uncle Averill Kaufman's hay field and into the woods, knowing that finding that dang dog would be like finding the proverbial needle in the haystack. After combing through the woods for three to four hours, I came upon him, his chain wrapped around a tree, hot and tired, with a guilty look on his face. He was at least a mile from the house. To this day I do not know why I headed the direction I did, or how I found him after searching only a very small fraction of the territory where he could have been trapped. It was either divine guidance or sheer luck.

In his later years Spot seemed to have given up on this escape attempts, having lost the desire to run, like the old prisoner fetching water for the "Boss" on the chain gang in "*Cool Hand Luke.*" And as Spot became more docile, I began to realize that he was now well past his prime. One summer day when he had been quite sick and listless for some time, I had decided to comfort Spot, realizing that I had practically forgotten about him for the last few weeks.

As I approached his doghouse, I became sickened by his condition. His eyes were fogged up with cataracts, and I knew that he could barely see. But even worse, I could see that poor Spot was miserably infested with fleas, the likes of which I had never seen. They literally crawled over his hair and flesh by the hundreds or perhaps thousands. Even the ground around his doghouse was infested, and I could see the fleas jumping on the bottom of my blue jean pants legs by the dozens as I stood and sadly thought about Spot's now miserable existence. Although my dad had tried to spray around Spot's house for fleas, whatever he had used was woefully inadequate for the task. We could not afford veterinarians or high priced medications, and I suppose my father could not bring himself to acknowledge that it was time to put down our faithful hound.

I sadly realized that Spot's life was no longer worth living. He would be better off dead than alive, and the way he looked up at me reinforced my decision. It was one of the hardest things I have ever done. Running back to the house, I hastily formulated a plan, grabbing a baseball bat and a shovel. I returned slowly, unsure whether I had the fortitude to put Spot out of his misery.

I could not stand the thought of Spot looking at me while I put him down. So I knelt beside him, and covered his cloudy eyes with my left hand. My mind worked against itself, for I didn't know if I could be so violent and yet so tenderly loving at the same time. Tears streaming down my face, I raised the bat with my right arm, hesitated for several seconds, and then brought the instrument down on his head as hard as I could. Unsure if I had killed him, I stood, then raised the bat and struck him another blow. I reached down to unfasten his collar, and then lovingly carried him to the fencerow behind the garden as I sobbed over his flea-infested body.

I dug a small grave, then after wrapping his body in a plastic bag I buried him. I laid a large rock over the small grave to prevent any animal from digging down to his body. I then walked to the barn, and finding two small boards, I crafted a rough cross, and pounded it into the ground behind the fresh grave. I bowed my head and said a prayer, thanking God for giving us such a wonderful hound, believing with all of my heart that I had done the right thing.

In many instances in life, doing the right thing is very difficult, and this was truly a hard lesson to learn at a young age, having to confront it in the way I did. This episode taught me that facing that difficulty head-on is the best course of action. To this day, I draw strength to face difficulties from the lesson learned.

The Vase

One summer my dad obtained a wooden swing and hung it from the rafters in our garage. During the hot summer months our friends would drop by, and we would sit in the swing, lined up three or four across, taking turns pushing each other in a steep arc toward the ceiling.

As we swang back and forth, we continually moved past a dusty ceramic vase, stashed on one of the many shelves my dad had created by nailing boards between the vertical two-by-four joists in the wall of the garage. For some reason it sat on that shelf for years, and was never selected for any of my mother's flower potting exercises. The small, squat vase was glazed with white paint, and in pea-green lettering was inscribed a lighthearted saying, "Be Happy, Be Gay, For Tomorrow Is Another Day."

My childhood, like the vase stashed on the shelf, remained encapsulated and untouched by news events and fads. Although I grew up in the turbulent 1960's and 1970's, I was in many ways sheltered from the turmoil happening in the world. I have no childhood recollection of the Vietnam War, the Beatles, the Rolling Stones, the controversy of school integration, marches, riots, or even the deaths of John Kennedy or Martin Luther King. For the most part, my friends and I were protected from such "adult" concerns by our parents and grandparents, who in those times spoke of such issues only in hushed tones among themselves. Rather, we were allowed to grow up without such burdens on our young shoulders, free to enjoy a life unencumbered with more mature concerns.

My children knew more in middle school about life, sex, war and the dangers around us than I knew in high school. I don't remember ever having a talk about "the birds and the bees" with either of my parents. On the rare occasions when an inappropriate word or joke crossed the airwaves as we watched television, my father would immediately get up out of his armchair and turn the television off. It is entirely different today, when even movies targeted to our children contain inappropriate comments, innuendos, and situations. I am embarrassed to admit that on many occasions I have been too lazy to follow the actions of my father, even with the convenience of a remote control. But on other occasions I have mustered the fortitude to change the channel or switch the television off, and on every such occasion I have remembered the parallel actions of my parents many years ago.

Today we congratulate ourselves for discussing mature issues openly with our children. And although I agree that this is for the best, I sometimes find myself questioning this approach, thinking back to those innocent times when we were blissfully unaware of the unrest and angst in that generation. And while I freely roamed the hills, roads and paths of rural West Virginia as a child, today we watch every movement of our children and hesitate to let them out of our sight.

That small vase was finally tossed out several years ago, discarded along with the innocence of those happier times, when words had different meanings than they do now. Its message of carefree happiness, appropriate for the time in which it was created, no longer applied, and took on an unsuitable overtone in the eyes of my parents. In many ways, that vase was a metaphor of a simpler time, and every now and then I remember when I shared the swing with my sisters and friends, our bare feet hanging in free air as we delightfully swung for hours on end; we were unencumbered by the harsh concerns of adulthood, and I wish I could return to that happy place just one more time.

The Accident

Averill Kaufman was our favorite uncle. First, because he lived just up the road from us, we saw him and were around him more frequently than our other uncles. As with all relationships, spending time with someone makes you comfortable with them, and we were certainly comfortable with Averill.

But mainly we liked Averill because of who he was. Averill had that gift of special attitude that only comes along every once in a while. Despite the circumstances he was in, he always was in a good mood, singing, whistling and humming as he went about life's daily duties. He loved to joke and kid around with us, and we enjoyed being around one who was so jovial and full of life's beans. A full time farmer and part-time bus driver, Averill typically tooled around his farm in coveralls and a conductor's hat, a product of the West Virginia countryside to the core. Averill loved life, and loved the people he shared it with, and in return we all loved him back. He was the husband of my mother's older sister, Geneva. My grandparents evidently had a sense of humor, because they named their daughters Geneva, Reva, and Eva. This pattern of names that rhymed but grew shorter was approaching the end of its possibilities, so they stopped having kids after my mother was born, or they might have been forced to name the next girl "Va."

Averill and Geneva lived in a large green farmhouse set high on a ridge, overlooking Route 68 and the valley below. On summer nights, the Kaufman family would gather on the front porch, pulling out guitars and banjos for an evening of country music and bluegrass entertainment. As a young child, I watched Geneva make homemade cottage cheese, amazed that out of the sharp smelling curdled milk she was able to get mild tasting cottage cheese. In the fall we would help

Averill load coal into his basement, as he filled up the coal room for firing the large furnace all winter long.

Set around their house were a variety of sheds, containing a mixture of tools, tractors, and farm implements, along with a large wooden barn that was usually filled to the top with bales of hay. As a child, I used to marvel at the construction of the barn, with it's large wooden beams set into joists that were carved into the vertical posts, all held in place by large wooden dowels.

The barn had two levels, and in the upper loft during the summer months, we stacked hay bales coming up the long conveyor. It was a horribly hot place to work, as the sun beat down on the tin roof without mercy. I preferred to work the other end of the wagon, loading bales on the conveyor as the ever-competitive Bobby Hoffman yelled down from the loft, "More Hay!", challenging us to a duel. We would bust our tails to keep the conveyor fully loaded, doing our best to bury those loft dwellers in an avalanche of hay. I still occasionally have surreal dreams in which I find myself in a massive wooden barn, a larger version of those I worked in during my youth, wandering around a mammoth upper loft, seemingly hundreds of feet long, that is filled with hay, tools, furniture, and other dusty remnants. For some reason the dream is always set at nighttime, the loft dimly lit by bare bulbs hanging in sockets, the stars shining down through the windows and cracks of the wooden boards that frame the structure.

In addition to his own farm, Averill helped his father Earl work his neighboring farm. A seasoned and well-oiled team, they worked together efficiently to manage their mix of crops and livestock; primarily cattle, turkeys, and hay. Most of their farmland was hilly, in contrast to the flat terrain of nearby farmers who worked the river-bottom land of the Ohio River. I was always convinced that this was a mark of toughness, and in some ways made them superior to their neighbors who were blessed with more fertile soil. Rather, they were toughened and honed by years of coaxing the hillsides to give all it had, working through the seasons to gratefully carve an existence from what God had given to them.

Averill owned two tractors, a red and white Massey Ferguson as well as an older model Allis Chalmers. The Allis was a "tricycle front end" machine, it's two small tires barely a foot across and overwhelmed by the two large tires in the rear. The burnt orange Allis was used for a variety of tasks: pulling wagons, mowing and raking hay, and moving dirt. Averill had a front-end loader that attached to the Allis, in which he could scoop up dirt to haul from one location to another, and then dump the soil and smooth it out with the blade on the front edge of the large bucket.

On the warm October 14 morning of 1978, shortly after my 16th birthday, I was playing around on the Ford tractor my father had recently purchased. We had a blade behind the tractor, and I was using it to move some gravel around on our driveway. This was more for the fun of it than anything else, as the driveway really didn't need the work, and gravel that was there was so packed down the blade was almost entirely ineffective. Our old Ford ran pretty well, but the brakes were practically non-existent, and you literally had to stand on the pedals to coax the old machine to a stop.

As I was playing around, our neighbor and minister's wife Enola Phillips ran up to the tractor with a fearful look on her face. I can still remember her exact words, "Geneva called. She thinks Averill's dead!" She then quickly told me he had apparently had an accident on his tractor, and she ran up to our house to give my mother the dreadful news.

I immediately took off on the tractor to Averill's house. I had no idea what I was going to do when I got there, but I wanted to get there quickly to see if there was any way I could assist if he was trapped or needed help. A lot of scenarios ran through my mind; perhaps I could pull the tractor off of him with our Ford tractor, or perhaps I could use the hydraulic blade lift to free him.

As I frantically drove up the short hill to their house, I was amazed to see that I was the first person to arrive. My aunt Geneva was standing in her back yard, at the crest of the hill, looking down into the hay field behind their house. She was too petrified to move, too terrified to go down to the accident scene. Her shaking body was frozen in place, unwilling to go down the hill for fear of what she would find and confirm at a closer vantage point. As I ran up to her, she simply said, "I think he's dead…"

I began running down the hill. As I approached the accident scene, I could see what had happened. Averill had been using the front loader on the Allis Chalmers, and the heavy load, combined with the narrow wheelbase on the front end, had created an unstable situation on the hillside and the tractor had overturned. As it overturned, it threw Averill downhill. He had landed on his stomach, and the flat frame above the rear tire had crashed down symmetrically on his back, the weight of the tractor pinning him to the ground.

The force of the tractor hitting him alone had probably killed him. If not, the weight of the tractor on his back would have prevented him from breathing. Either way, the pressure on his body forced blood to his face and arms, which were already a deep and unnatural shade of purple. As I approached and knelt down next to him, I realized that he was already dead, and knew there was no way to save him.

The weight of the entire situation hit me as I knelt there beside his body. Geneva had lost her husband. Earl and Lena Kaufman had lost their only child. My cousins, now grown and married, had lost their father, and their children had lost a grandfather. My mother and other aunts and uncles had lost a brother. And our community had lost a pillar, a beloved man who was an interwoven part of the fabric of the neighborhood of Hopewell Hill.

When Geneva and Averill woke up that morning, they had every reason to think that this was going to be "just another day." We tend to discount the likelihood that terrible events will befall us, and even in the face of aging and death we tend to think that at least for the present time, we are in a way immortal. But death can come at any time, and it never comes easily for those left behind, especially when unexpected. Our only solace was in the fact that Averill was a faithful Christian, a fine man, who in his death was released from this world to a more perfect home above.

I looked back up the hill and saw my aunt Geneva standing there, some 50 yards away, her hands clasped together, the wind rippling her sundress as she looked down toward me for some indication of what I had found. It was up to me to tell her the terrible news, that Averill was dead. I felt as if I aged years in those few seconds, as I knelt beside my dead uncle in the short October grass, and wondered what I would say to my aunt. I dreaded it, and felt completely unprepared to deal with the situation. But I knew it had to be done. I began the long walk up the hill, knowing that I would be the one to confirm her worst fears. For all of us who knew and loved Averill, life on Hopewell Hill would never be the same.

Death on Hopewell Curve

We were periodically exposed to traffic accidents on Route 68, the two-lane road that ran in front of our house. After topping off on top of the hill, the road begins a long decline as you head north toward Parkersburg. The top of the hill is fairly straight and flat for about half of a mile, and the long descent is also straight. But the transition involves a fairly broad curve. This is a recipe for disaster, because some drivers underestimate the ability of their vehicles to make the curve at high speeds.

One summer day, a small pickup blew past our house, heading for the downhill curve at a high rate of speed with no lights on as dusk began settling into warm summer nightfall. Although hundreds of cars passed our house every day, this one caught our attention due to the surreal rate of speed at which it was heading down the road. We were used to cars traveling fast on the two-lane blacktop road, but this was beyond ordinary, and the high-pitched sound from the engine caught our attention.

Although I did not see the wreck, the sound of the crash carried loudly to our house, and we immediately began running to the scene of the accident. The wreck had occurred around the bend, out of the line-of—sight of our yard, so we had to run quite a distance to get to the location of the vehicle. The driver had lost control of the truck in the curve and swerved too hard to overcorrect, causing the truck to oscillate and flip onto its roof as it slid off of the road and into a ditch. As I approached, I heard the sound of three teenage boys screaming out in panic. When the truck flipped and slid, the roof crushed downward enough to trap the boys inside. By the time we got to the scene, the truck was engulfed in flames—the gas tank had severed. Along with

15

other bystanders, we watched helplessly as the flames roared out of control. It was way too hot to approach the truck, and the flames shot up so quickly that no rescue attempt was possible.

It's a terrible feeling, hearing the screams of young men who are being burned alive, and being unable to do anything to help them. Some of the bystanders ran around in a frantic and futile search for fire extinguishers, while others just stared in unbelief at the scene unfolding before their eyes. Other turned their heads or covered their ears. Before long, the screams grew silent, and we knew it was too late to help the poor souls who died that evening. An eerie hush fell over the scene, before the silence was again broken by the sound of approaching sirens.

This incident hit me hard, not just due to the graphic nature of the event, but because the boys who died were young, about my age at the time. With a single miscalculation, the driver and his two friends suffered a horrid and tragic death. It was a poignant reminder of the frailty of life, the potential seriousness of the consequences of our actions, and the capability of death to come suddenly and without warning when we least expect it.

The Great Chinchilla Caper of 1974

My grandfather Charles Ray Dowler was an electrician by trade, but he had retired long before I could remember, and was now in my mind simply a world-class tinkerer. "Gramps", as we affectionately called him, spent hours upon end in his garage workshop, building, fixing and adapting most anything. He did not have the best-equipped workshop I had ever seen, but he had a way of using the tools he had very resourcefully.

Furthermore, Gramps was known for miles around for his clock repairing abilities. He savored tearing into old German clocks, carefully examining the springs, movements, and wooden gears, using all of his skills to adjust, oil, repair, or craft new pieces to revive the old masterpieces. His knowledge of old clocks was amazing, and he admired the handiwork of those German engineered clocks, especially Cuckoo clocks. My grandparent's house was a fascinating place at Noon, as dozens of clocks, all carefully timed, would begin to chime, ring, dong and cuckoo within seconds of each other, putting on a concerto for the better part of a minute. My parents and Granny, refined by years from the insanity of dealing with this clock cacophony, would stop all conversations, patiently waiting out this assault on the senses, resuming the conversation only after the last clock had finished announcing the time.

Our ever resourceful Gramps and Granny came to dinner one night, bursting at the seams with excitement, having hinted that they were going to let us in on a great opportunity. They had come across a sure-fire way to make lots of extra cash. Not having a lot of the green stuff either, we were ripe for the plucking, and presented them with a most willing audience. Gramps announced that he had found a great business venture, and even though it required some investment up front, it would quickly return that investment and more. This great opportunity, they announced, was in raising chinchillas.

Barely able to contain our excitement, we looked at each other and exclaimed, "Raising chinchillas! Of course! Why hadn't we thought of that ourselves?" After the initial euphoria sunk in, we realized we were overlooking one small item—we had no idea what a chinchilla was, although we suspected it might be in some way related to a llama. After we settled down, Gramps carefully explained that chinchillas were small rodents, valued for their fine fur. Chinchillas are so small, yet their hair so long and fine, that if you close your eyes and hold out your hand, someone can take a chinchilla, turn it on it's back, rub the fur on your palm for a few strokes, then lay it into your hand and you cannot even tell it is there.

In our excitement, we all were talking at once, speculating about this idea of a chinchilla farm. Gramps settled down enough to teach us what he knew. Chinchillas, he told us, are notoriously picky eaters, requiring carefully measured daily doses of seeds, alfalfa and fine hay. Of course I understood this perfectly, as I would not eat anything that was mashed or covered with gravy, and refused to eat at all if any food item contacted another on my plate. In the wild, chinchillas are known to eat insects and bird eggs, but that was beyond our means of supply. In captivity, they eat their food a little at a time, not all at once. Consequently you will see them come out periodically through the day to feed.

Chinchillas have a long and distinguished history. They are almost certainly descendants of pre-historic chin like animals called Megamys. In the wild, they have not ventured outside the area in which they were originally found, the semi-arid areas of the Andes Mountains in Argentina, Bolivia, Chile and Peru. When the Spaniards traveled to South America in 1524, they encountered a tribe of Indians called Chinchas, who introduced them to the little furry animals. The Chinchas wore their pelts and at the same time kept them as pets. The Spaniards named the animals the "chinchilla" after the Indian tribe—the word literally means "Little Chinchas". They took pelts back with them to Europe and started the Chin fur business. Now, 450 years later, we were ready to continue the tradition and hop onto this gravy train.

Now we understood his proposal—that we raise chinchillas and sell them for their fur. This was before fur coats were politically incorrect, and in the early 1970's women would pay thousands of dollars for a chinchilla fur coat, the creme de la creme of all furs. We were somewhat familiar with the fur industry, as several of our neighbors would occasionally trap foxes, selling their furs for decent money. We decided right then and there that we were in on this exotic adventure, and we already had dreams of becoming rich from raising chinchillas.

There was only one small problem. Chinchillas are picky, and their living climate must be carefully controlled. Unfortunately, we could not cage them up outside or in the barn, nor could we allow them to freely roam the yard, picking up seeds, nuts and small insects like a free-range chicken. Rather, they had to stay inside the house where they would be "comfortable". Stressing them out, in addition to potentially causing their fur to fall out, might also affect their mating habits. I surmised that in that manner they were very much like humans.

Because our ranch house had a generous and fairly dry basement, it was quickly agreed that this was the place to "temporarily" establish the chinchilla farm. Our plan, after the profits started rolling in, was to build a carefully constructed, climate-controlled chinchilla facility, with enough money left over to shred dollar bills to line the cages. We even visited such a facility in Indiana, carefully doing our research before finally committing to this enterprise. Here, chinchillas were being raised by the hundreds, and the "farmers" agreed that they could spare some of their stock to sell to us to start our own operation.

A deal was struck, and one corner of our basement was transformed. Walls and lights went up, and special cages were imported to house our valuable new "livestock". Chinchilla cages are built in rows, each individual unit being approximately 2 feet by 3 feet and 18 inches high, and constructed from wire mesh. A special "run" is constructed that connects about four of the cages in the back, with a round access hole leading to each of the individual units. The cages take advantage of the fact that the males are smaller than the females. Thus, one male can squeeze through the access holes into the run, freely entering any of the cages, each of which is occupied by a female chinchilla.

The operation finally ready, we purchased several chinchillas, and brought them to their new home. We waited for the babies to start appearing. And waited. And waited. But the babies never came. We knew they were fickle, but this was ridiculous. "What are we doing wrong?" we asked ourselves, and while dad and Gramps experimented with lighting, food, climate control and other variables, we could never get the animals to breed. They even experimented with matchmaking, putting different males with the females, much like Chuck Woolery in *The Dating Game*. But nothing worked.

Me, well, I was convinced it was all in the cage arrangement. First of all, each male had access to four females. Which didn't sound bad if you were the male, but the females were no doubt too jealous with each other to ever be in the mood for romance. Besides, there was only wire mesh between the cages, and every move of the male could be monitored by all of the females on a 24-hour basis. Even if one of the females was in the mood for a romantic liaison, they had no privacy. The male chinchilla had to be a nervous wreck, and it was no wonder that baby chinchillas were not appearing.

After several months of this futility, my dad and Gramps decided that their business venture was regretfully a bust. The chinchillas were sent back to Indiana, no doubt at a steep discount to the initial buying price. The cages were dismantled, and all we ended up with was a new room in our basement. Which was not a total loss, as it made a great workshop.

We learned a valuable lesson from this chapter of our lives, that if things look too good to be true, they probably are. I suspect that the "farmers" who sold Gramps on this plan knew from the start that it was likely to fail, and suckered us into buying animals, cages and other equipment at a high markup, no doubt repeating this exercise on many other unsuspecting would-be entrepreneurs. And just like the Andean Indians, we ended up on the short end of the stick. I have no idea how much money we lost on this business deal, but as with any failed venture, the financial losses are somewhat tempered by a gain in experience and wisdom. We came out of it somewhat embarrassed, but wiser for the wear. Perhaps someday I'll commission a special tee shirt for my dad, "I Survived The Great Chinchilla Caper Of 1974."

Bread Truck Camper

After his retirement, Gramps bounced around from project to project. Not one to retire to a rocking chair, he instead found a new life as a handyman, clock repairman, and jack of all trades, and he attacked each with gusto, as if he was wound as tight as the springs in some of his antique German clocks.

Despite his age, Gramps got around quite well, and was really a tough old bird. One example of his strong nature was his survival of a hunting accident early in his life. After a hunting trip, his hunting buddy accidentally shot Gramps in the jaw while unloading his rifle. Gramps was rushed to the hospital. The wound itself was not life threatening, but infection set in, and a high fever ensued. The doctors ordered that he be moved to the basement of the hospital, which is where they put patients who were about to die in those days. Gramps may have been down, but he was definitely not out. Knowing that with the move to the basement they were effectively giving up on him, he ordered the nurses to bring him a pile of blankets, and began sweating it out on his own. It must have been a tough couple of days for him, but he finally broke the fever, the first step in his complete recovery.

After several years of honing his handyman skills, he embarked on the mother of all projects one summer, announcing that he was going to take an old delivery truck and turn it into a camper. We were a little bit skeptical, until we drove into town on Saturday to see the vehicle he had purchased for this project. Then we were very skeptical. The truck looked worse for the wear, the paint faded over the aluminum shell, and the fabric of the drivers seat ripped and torn. It was one of those trucks with a sliding drivers side door, so the deliveryman could quickly jump off the seat, which was simply elevated on a pole above the floor of the truck. I knew one thing was certain, that Granny would never drive this vehicle. Standing a little over 5 feet tall, there was no way that her feet could reach the pedals. I quickly decided there was no way I would ever go on vacation in a vehicle with "Stork Bread Company" painted on the sides—people would likely think we were the Trapp family of delivery, and would likely be confused to whether we were bringing babies or loaves of Wonder Bread.

But where we saw an old delivery truck, Gramps saw a prime recreational vehicle, and he attacked the project with vigor. He started with the motor, getting a mechanic to give her a complete overhaul. He then decided the truck was too small for his "camper" plans, so he extended the box frame by four feet in the back. Buying an assortment of items, like a sink, refrigerator, and gas stove, he incorporated them into the vehicle, then made all of the furniture and cabinets, and even did the plumbing and wiring himself. From time to time he would enlist my dad to help out, pulling him into his plans when he had a job that needed more than one set of hands. He even put in additional windows, a tiny bathroom, and regular doors. Fortunately, he decided to paint the camper. Unfortunately, he chose a metallic gold color. It looked like he was preparing for a trip to Las Vegas. I could almost picture him pulling up to the Sands Hotel wearing a sequined Elvis suit and sunglasses.

After months of work the camper was finally finished. And although he did surprisingly well, considering that almost everything was put together and crafted by hand, the camper definitely had the look of an amateur job. He didn't mind, as it was functional, and he could drive it to Florida in the winter, probably with the turn signal on the whole way. For gramps, Florida was Heaven on earth, where he would surf fish while Granny crocheted, sewed and made crafts out of seashells for hours on end.

The summer after my third grade year, my dad made arrangements to borrow the camper for a week so we could take a trip to the beach. We looked forward to this week long vacation, which was a rare event in our household, and I remember taking only a few such trips during my entire childhood. Rather, most of my dad's vacation time was spent working around our house, focused on the myriad of tasks that surround anyone who lives on a small farm. So it was with great anticipation that we packed the camper full of food, clothes, toys and other necessities, finally pulling out in our humble ride as we embarked toward the Outer Banks of North Carolina.

I have surprising few memories of that trip, but can still muster up images of the Wright Brothers plane at Kitty Hawk, and remember watching men jump off the windy dunes in colorful hang gliders. I can recall clawing my way to the tops of the dunes, watching the wind rapidly work to cover up my tracks, as if it were in some way embarrassed at the desecration imprinted by my footsteps. We visited several lighthouses, and I can still remember being amazed at the size and strength of these structures.

However, I guess it is human nature to remember the negative images more strongly than the positive; thus I have strong memories of that trip of things that did not go well. For example, the camper got stuck at one of the beachside campsites, tires spitting sand angrily as my dad punched the accelerator over and over in an attempt to claw his way to freedom. Fortunately for us, someone came to our aid, pulling us out of our rut with a CJ Jeep.

I can also remember those summer nights, when it was too hot in the camper to sleep. We sweated and laid in misery as the summer breeze tried in vain to force its way through the ridiculously small windows my grandfather had installed. Worst of all, Gramps had undersized the bathroom ventilation, and the smell of the sewage tank permeated the thick night air, piling misery upon misery until my mother was ready to pack it up and come home early. Somehow we made it through each night, fitfully sleeping until finally welcoming the arrival of morning and the fresh outdoor air with a renewed appreciation.

During our return trip, my father got the brilliant idea that the perfect way to cap off our vacation would be to drive to the bottom of the New River Gorge arch bridge in Fayetteville, West Virginia. It was not enough for him to view the bridge from the overlooks at the upper level, marveling at the 1700-foot span across the steep gorge carved between the mountains by the rushing white water of the New River. Here, we could admire the views from above while reading the placards touting interesting facts about this engineering marvel. For example, that it reduced a 40-minute drive to less than a minute, and that it weighed more than 4000 elephants, as if this was suddenly an internationally recognized unit of measurement.

Instead, dad decided that we would get a much better view if we drove to the river level, some 876 feet below the flat top of the bridge, observing the wonders of the bridge as it towered above us. So we began our descent downward, winding down the curvy mountain roads as we made our way toward the bottom. Not too long after beginning our decline, it became obvious that we were hopelessly outclassed. As the brakes in the van heated and began to smell, my dad furiously manipulated the stick shift and fought the steering wheel. The bends got tighter and tighter, as if mocking my dad, but there was no way to turn around, nowhere to go but downhill, as if we were sucked into a cruel and mocking downward spiral. As we spiraled downward in the hot, overheated camper, I can still picture the sweat oozing from dads forehead, beading up and rolling down his face, finally dropping like rain to soak his shirt. Finally we reached the bottom, and we found a place barely big enough to turn the camper around. The trip back up the mountain was just as stressful, the motor straining to pull the weight of the camper up the twisted mountain roads. Finally, reaching the safety of Route 19, we breathed a sigh of relief and continued homeward.

That was the last time we took the camper out. Gramps continued to drive the camper for many years after that, but we willingly ceded it back to him for his exclusive purposes.

The camper actually did quite well, considering its humble beginnings and the original purpose of that modified bread delivery truck, but it was as if we could not stomach any more excitement.

As is often the case, my dad had good intentions, wanting to allow us to wonder at the marvels of the arch bridge with a unique perspective at the river level. This was the road less traveled, a path for the brave, intended to be an adventure for us. Funny, I cannot remember an image of that bridge from below. But I have a more precious image locked into my memory, that of my father, soaked with sweat and concentration at the highest possible level, battling the stick shift, clutch, brakes and steering wheel of the camper, working valiantly and somewhat fearfully to bring us all of out of that canyon to safety.

My Grandfather's Vehicles

In his later years, my grandfather Ray Dowler acquired an eclectic mix of vehicles. In addition to the bread truck camper, Gramps also purchased an International Scout and much to our surprise, a purple dune buggy. For some reason, Granny tolerated his late-life freewheeling spending pattern, as if finally allowing him to act out on a long-suppressed mid-life crisis. And while he kept the dune buggy at his house, he allowed us to keep the Scout at our place.

The International Scout was a true four-wheel drive vehicle, seemingly styled after the Land Rovers I had seen in childhood movies of African safaris. The Scout was light blue with a white top, and had only the essentials, from its stark interior and standard transmission to the dashboard, which contained only a few instruments. As if to add insult to injury, the gas gauge did not work. Never knowing how much gas was in the tank was a true adventure. Not wanting to get stranded, I routinely stopped to fill up the tank every time I drove it to high school. On one occasion I stopped, told the clerk to fill it up, and he came back in about one minute and asked for 50 cents!

The Scout was hard to drive, with a standard stick-shift transmission, and it did not contain power steering. Furthermore, there was such slop in the rack and pinion steering mechanism that just keeping the old vehicle in a straight line on the highway was a real chore. To make a slight correction to the left, you had to turn the wheel a quarter turn or so just to tighten up the steering rack, then give it a small but firm tug past that point. Then you inevitably had to do the same in the opposite direction just a few seconds later. It was quite frustrating, engaging in this repetitive back and forth dance just to keep going in a straight line. Going around a curve was actually quite a relief, as you could finally hold the steering steady, even if only for just a few seconds.

I really learned how to drive in the Scout. On one wintry day, I picked up my friend Eric Bradley in the Scout for a ride to school. I was, at that time, still a novice at driving. I pulled out of our driveway onto Rt. 68 and "goosed" the gas a bit on the downward sloping snow-covered road. In no time we were in the midst of a 360-degree turn in the middle of the highway! When we stopped we were headed in the right direction, but it was a good thing there was little or no traffic that day. I have no idea why my parents let me drive to school on such a wintry day. On another occasion, coming home late at night, I "forgot" that a left turn has to yield on green, and almost caused a car to plow into me at a very high rate of speed as I turned from route 95 onto route 68 at the "Dupont" intersection. It was such a narrow miss, and one so frightening, that after it happened the other driver and I both squealed to a stop and had to sit there for several minutes to calm our nerves enough to get back on the road and drive on. Like many who have made it through the teenage years, it's a wonder that I'm still alive.

Sometimes for fun, my dad would let us drive the Scout around the garden and through the orchard. My sister Leslie and I would take turns driving, while our friends rode circles around us on bicycles or ran alongside us. Not too long after my grandfather had purchased the Scout, Leslie made a miscalculation and ended up slamming the front end into an apple tree. There, in the front of the hood, was a rather large and permanent indentation. This is one of the occasions where I remember my father being truly angry. He did not look forward to explaining that the Scout had been damaged because we were goofing off and driving it through the orchard. I was just glad it was her and not me.

One summer, after noticing the many rust holes and spots on the Scout, I decided to give her a paint job. I found a gallon of body putty, some sanding paper, and a leftover gallon of gold speckled paint from when Gramps had painted his camper. Ready to begin, I proceeded to clean out the rusted spots with a wire brush, and then began applying thick layers of putty. After sanding the putty smooth, I masked off the old Scout, then proceeded to cover up the blue and white with shiny speckled gold. It was without a doubt the worst body repair and paint job in the history of automotive travel. The putty bulged out in places, and though sanded smooth, protruded in and out of the natural curves of the sheet metal. The paint was rough instead of smooth, as though it had been applied with small gritty sand mixed into it. And in some places there were runs in the paint, or marks where I had accidentally brushed against the Scout while painting.

When he inspected my handiwork, Gramps made a big deal about how much he liked the new look for the Scout. To this day, I have no idea if he genuinely liked it, or was just saying that to make me feel better. I guess it looked okay from afar, and that was good enough for him. If nothing else, it was a valuable experience that taught me not to pursue a career in the automotive repair industry.

To my parents, the purchase of the Scout was an understandable lapse in my grandfather's judgment. But the dune buggy, that was a completely different matter. Granny and Gramps were as out of place in the dune buggy as Ronald Reagan was at a "Friends of Communism" convention. With its fiberglass body painted metallic purple, oversized wheels, and rear-mounted motor with chromed exhaust pipes, the buggy was the coolest vehicle my sisters and I had ever seen. It was like something out of hot rod magazine. Unfortunately, Gramps wisely kept a much tighter control on his dune buggy than the Scout. I can only remember taking one short ride in this magical vehicle. When he had the buggy in town, he kept it in his garage under lock and key

One year he towed it to Florida behind his camper, he left it there for a few years then finally sold it. In my mind's eye I could see a surreal image of my grandparents in Florida, cruising the strip at Daytona beach, my grandfather proudly driving along as Granny sat in the passenger seat unemotionally stitching up a doily or one of those monkeys you make out of a big gray sock with the red heel for the mouth.

I often wondered how he felt when he sold it, after realizing that it was not a good "fit" to his more sedate lifestyle. I expect this was a very sad occasion for him, though he would not have showed it. Gramps made a common mistake: trying to hold onto youth for too long. For some of us, it involves playing sports well past our prime, only to be reminded by sore muscles or injuries that our bodies are no longer as spry as they once were. For others, it involves makeup, constantly shifting hairstyles, or even cosmetic surgery. Some men even ditch their spouses, and look for a younger "trophy" wife to hang on their arms in their later years. In retrospect, Gramps obsession with sporty vehicles was a much more forgiving and healthy behavior, and we readily forgave him.

Joey and the Feisty Holstein

Each summer, the Wood County 4-H Fair and Interstate Exhibition colored the landscape of my childhood. Of course, no one but the people who published the annual fair brochure called it that. Everyone else in Wood County just called it the Wood County Fair, or better yet, "The Fair" and anyone on this side of the Ohio River knew what we meant. Any farmer worth his salt who was asked, "Whatcha takin' to th' Fair this year" could instantly muster up an appropriate response. Maybe it sounded more impressive to give it a large name. But with that logic, we wondered why they didn't go ahead and call it something like the Grand Wood County International 4-H Fair and Interstate Extravaganza Supreme.

One summer, our next-door neighbors, Jim and Enola Phillips, found themselves in a bind as a result of the fair; their daughter Lori won a Holstein calf there. Lori and Beth Sellers, her best friend that particular summer, had plotted a grand "ballot stuffing" scheme, which was implemented under the unsuspecting watch of the local chapter of the Modern Woodmen's Club of Wood County. While the Woodmen were no doubt distracted by the Daughters of the American Revolution, who had a booth just across the aisle, Lori and Beth repeatedly stuffed ballots by the dozens into the box every time they walked by their booth. Not surprisingly, one of the hundreds of ballots Lori and Beth had stuffed into the drawing box was pulled out in the drawing on the last day of the fair. Fortunately for Lori they offered only one grand prize, and no consolation prizes, or her scheme would have been uncovered, no-doubt casting a shadow over Jim's career in the ministry. And so, Lori was now the proud owner of a feisty Holstein calf. This presented a slight problem, because Jim was the local minister of the Hopewell Church of Christ, and he and his wife Enola raised their four children in the church "parsonage." They owned no land at all, only having the use of the fourth-acre lot occupied by the house.

Since we lived next to them, just across from the Hopewell cemetery, my dad was asked if he "minded" allowing them to raise the calf in our pasture for the summer, at least until the calf was old enough to butcher. We didn't know whether to be irritated or amused, and ended up settling for a little of both. First, we were irritated, not so much at Jim for asking, but at my dad, who has such a large heart that he can't say no to anyone. We were just glad Lori hadn't won something like a herd of goats, ostriches or emus, because had they asked my dad, we would have ended up keeping the whole lot of them on our place for the summer as well.

Second, we were amused, as every full or even part-time farmer worth his salt knows you don't raise a Holstein for butchering. Holsteins have been bred, refined and optimized for thousands of years into lean, mean milk-producing machines. Their back hip bones stick up into the air as if unencumbered by the few pounds of muscle in their legs, and appear as though they will burst out of their stretched-out hide at any minute. Their gaunt build and oversized gut leads one to believe that after skinning out a 750 pound yearling you would have a good 50 pounds of stringy meat on the hook, if you were lucky. Even the black spots on their white coats imply they were made for white and chocolate milk production, as opposed to prime rib, New York strip or the other fine cuts of beef that they were no doubt dreaming about in the Phillips household.

In our part of Wood County, the prevailing attitude was that the best breeds for the production of fine, marbled meat were either Charolais or Angus steers, and many a heated discussion was held between farmers on which actually was the best. Every truck had at least one bumper sticker touting the benefits of the driver's favorite breed. A few people in the northern edges of the county favored Herefords, but we looked down on that particular breed with a confident air of superiority. Some of the larger farms were bringing in a breed called Limousines, a supposedly "superior" crossbreed with the best characteristics of several lines, but we figured any steer named after a fancy automobile had no place in our part of the county. One thing we all agreed upon was that while Holsteins were unsurpassed for dairy operations, even Herefords were miles ahead of them for the production of meat. None of this seemed to register with the our minister and his family, which was not surprising to us—they had come to rural Wood County from "the city" and simply didn't know any better. We couldn't hold it against them.

And so, Lori Phillip's Holstein calf became our squatter for the summer. Having only squatter's rights, the calf was shut out of the barn, away from the larger steers, and had only the pasture and a small corner shed for protection. Despite the fact that is was his sister Lori who had won this prize animal, it was my friend Joey who drew the short end of the stick and more often than not had to trek over to our house to feed the calf. To feed the calf, Joey had to walk to our barn, fill a small pail with feed, and haul it to the corner shed.

It was on one such occasion that my skinny friend learned the hard way how feisty a small Holstein calf can be. Having finished his daily chore, Joey began walking back across the field toward our house, swinging his empty bucket. I don't know what got into the calf, perhaps it somehow figured out the injustice of its situation, a dairy specialist doomed to meat production at the hands of our unknowledgeable neighbors. But something got into the normally docile beast, and it took off running toward Joey. As it approached my friend, the calf positioned its head at his posterior, and with a forceful upward swing lifted Joey completely off of the ground. Joey went flying forward, somehow miraculously landing on his feet. With a look of horror on his face, he hit the ground running, making a beeline for the pasture gate.

As he raced toward the gate, the scene repeated itself over and over. Joey ran a few steps, and then the calf would catch up to him and lift his lithe body completely off the ground with a firm head butt. He would go up into the air, arms and legs flying, and then somehow hit the ground running a few more steps. I had never laughed so hard in my young existence, seeing this comical scene played out in front of me. I don't know what was most amazing, that Joey made it to the gate without falling down, or that he mindlessly held onto the bucket through each assisted leap. Finally, he reached the gate and in a blind panic climbed over it to safety. I wish I had a video of that event, for I would never tire of watching it, and it would easily win a sizeable prize on America's Funniest Home Videos.

From that point forward, a large stick was added to the list of essential tools required for feeding the Holstein. The calf, after several more months, finally made it to the Phillips dinner table, and I have no doubt that Joey greatly enjoyed that first meal, each bite important to winning back part of his bruised and shattered dignity. I just wonder if he was sitting on a pillow when he savored that first stringy bite of Holstein delicacy.

The Case of the Drunken 4-H Judge

In the traditional suburbs, children benefit from a smorgasbord of activities—a variety of organized sports, like soccer, baseball and football, and church trips, camps, clubs, brownies, scouts, and so on. As a child, I used to longingly dream of participating in such activities. But, due to my father's shift work schedules, the distance from most of these activities, and the demands of a country lifestyle, we did not get to participate in many of these time-demanding activities. Our parents allowed us to pick from a list of one, so we selected what was available—the Daniel Boone 4-H Club.

Our 4-H club met in Belleville, in a block building that had recently been constructed, which was actually a pretty nice facility. The construction of this facility was made possible by a hastily formed alliance with the Wood County Coon Hunters Association, who also needed a place to hang out, and who fortunately did most of the work. Every month, we would faithfully attend our meeting, promising to honor and improve the four H's of head, heart, hands and health, as our long-time leader Nadine puffed away at a cigarette during our pledge recital.

The culmination of every 4-H activity is the county fair. We traditionally did many projects, in areas such as photography, crafts and health, but for my sister Leslie and I, the important activity was the 4-H baby beef steer project. The steer was called a baby, but our yearlings typically reached weights of well over 1000 lbs., and could be quite a handful. In the baby beef project, not only do you have to raise a good steer, but you have to train them as well. Our steers were typically as tame as a housecat; we taught them to lead around on a leash, and they were washed, groomed, and even taught how to stand for best show-manship. All of this takes a lot of time and patience, as well as knowing the tricks of the trade.

The training starts as soon as you get the young calves. We usually got ours from Jim Miller, who had a Charolais farm a few miles from our house. He loved the publicity that providing good steers brought, but his sons were too young to participate. So he would sell us two of his best bull calves each year. Upon arrival, you begin immediately to "bond" with the calves, feeding them, brushing them, and putting rings in their nose to teach them to respect the lead ropes. Once that was accomplished, the rings would be removed and harnesses put on. Usually we would allow a rope to drag the ground from the har-ness—when the calf stepped on the rope, it tightened the harness, pull-ing on a chain running through the calf's mouth. This was also effective in teaching them to respect the lead rope.

We also used "goad" sticks to train the animals to stand with all four legs squarely underneath their bodies. These sticks were pointed, but also had a nail that passed through close to the tip. This nail served two purposes—it allowed you to pull back on a leg that was out too far, causing the animal to move it to the proper location. It was also used to scratch the animal's bellies when they were standing properly, which was a reward for proper posture. All of this requires hours and hours of training.

Just as you were developing a relationship, it was time to castrate and dehorn the calves, and the animal's trust took a giant step back-wards. Taking proper veterinary care of a calf is a big and very interest-ing chore. The first step is to "shoo" the animal into a narrow stall, and when the calf's head pokes through the opening on the other side, a board is pushed sideways to tightly clamp alongside its neck. The cas-tration is quite simple—a special device stretches out a small rubber band, which is slipped over the calf's testicles and triggered, snapping the rubber band shut. This cuts off all circulation, and in a week or so everything "falls off"—hopefully out in a field somewhere, where you won't have to see it. The dehorning is much more interesting. In this task, a special pair of cutters is attached to two long wooden handles. This is placed over the small horn, and then the cutters are forcibly closed, digging down into the scalp and cutting through the soft base of the horn with a sickening cutting sound. The horn falls away, and blood spurts out through severed vessels until a special powder is applied, causing fast clotting.

On a few occasions our calves got "warbles", large grub-like worms that formed below the skin. These we left alone until they were "ripe", kind of like a nice zit. Then, we would take a glass pop bottle, place the opening over the warble, and pop our fists down on the bottom of the bottle, popping the warble out of the sore in the hide and into the bottle.

At the county fair, there are really two competitions in the baby beef project. The first is when the animals are judged for build, leanness and muscle content. The second competition is showmanship, where the young showmen are judged on their abilities to lead, groom, and control their animals. During one showmanship competition my steer got spooked, and began running wildly around the ring. I held onto the lead rope for dear life, knowing that losing the animal would be a sure blow to any chances I had to a showmanship ribbon. As the steer effortlessly dragged all 98 pounds of my skinny frame around the ring, my mother kept shouting, "Let go! Let go!" as I hung on for dear life. Finally, after what seemed to be an eternity, the animal quieted down, and I led him back to his spot in the show ring. The judge, no doubt amused at the comical sight of a spectacled 6th grade kid being tossed around the ring, took pity on me and gave me second place in showmanship that year.

This is heady stuff for a 12-year-old kid—parading around a large animal in front of a few hundred people, and receiving ribbons, trophies, and applause. This event is the highlight of the show ring, surpassing even the greased pole climb and the female tobacco-spitting contest. The final parade through the ring is the auction, where bidders compete to buy the steers, primarily as a means of getting publicity for their local businesses while doing good for local kids and the communities. We made pretty decent money on our steers, and it gave us a good start on our college savings. Occasionally, the buyers would donate the steers back to the 4-H organization, allowing them to raise money by butchering the steers and cooking them in a large charcoal pit for a "steer roast." We would buy tickets then attend the roast, the whole time wondering if we were eating our own steer, which had been like a friendly family pet only a week before. It was a weird feeling, eating an animal that you had raised, trained and even named. Many of the girls couldn't bring themselves to participate in the roast—it was just too much.

Leslie and I raised steers for the county fair for six consecutive years. We were very successful—during two of those years my steer was proclaimed the Grand Champion, and during two of those years Leslie's steer won Grand Champion. One of the years we decided not to take our steers, because they got a bad case of warts on their heads. This did not affect their ability to be sold and slaughtered, but we just did not feel right showing them in competition. This was very depressing for us, because we were getting used to the glory and high selling price that the top steers bring at the fair.

Thus, there was only one year when we went to the fair and did not win the top prize. That year, it was widely known and whispered among the barns at the fair that the contest was rigged. The farmers who raised Herefords were getting tired of losing to a Charolais steer each year. The people who brought in the judges were members of the Hereford crowd, and they decided to bring in a ringer. It was known before the judging even began that a Hereford steer would win the top prizes that year, no matter which animals were really the best.

As we led our steers into the show ring, we anxiously looked at the man who would be judging the steers. As he moved from animal to animal, putting on a "show" of feeling and eyeing the animals, it became apparent that he was struggling. As he stumbled around the ring, it soon became obvious to the crowd that not only was he biased, he was very much under the influence of alcohol! Nevertheless, he was sober enough to pick Hereford steers for the top spots, probably in line with a list that had been developed previously. It was a sham, and very visible for everyone to see.

We learned a very valuable lesson that year. Conflicts in judging don't just happen in Olympic ice-skating—they occur everywhere, to ordinary people like you and me. Even when the entire event is for the benefit of children, the pride of parents and the others involved can lead them to resort to unfairness and fraud. We see this all of the time, in situations where parents fight at little league games and angry moms kick dirt at umpires. But it sometimes goes beyond the sports field, to the classrooms and offices we occupy.

All of the kids, even the ones who owned Herefords, were disgusted at the whole affair that year. We just wanted to show our steers in a fair environment, and let the chips fall where they may. But life is not always fair, and the drunken 4-H judge was an eye-opening introduction to that realization.

Tobacco Spittin' Girls

Money can disappear incredibly fast from the pocket of a young boy at a county fair. In addition to the irresistible carnival games and side-shows, it seemed that every non-profit group in Wood County had a tent at the fair, where they sold homemade ice cream, hot dogs, sausages, crafts, toys or any other item that people had shown a previous willingness to shell out money to buy. So by 9 a.m. we were usually broke, and we had to look for low-budget or free ways to keep ourselves occupied until our parents could be persuaded to cough up more money.

I suppose every county fair in the United States has the same tried-and-true events, like chainsaw cutting contests, strong man competitions, tractor pulls, demolition derbies, greased pole climbs, and greased pig catching contests. I was terrible at the grease pole climb. In this contest, the bark is stripped off of a long straight tree trunk, then it is planted in the ground and the already slick green wood is greased up with a generous dose of cooking oil. The top of the pole has a $50 bill attached, and the first person to climb all the way to the top gets to keep the money he or she snags. At first, a large rag-tag group of competitors lines up to go after the prize money. No one wants to go early, because they will be forced to "absorb" a generous portion of the oil. So a lot of line shuffling takes place, as each contestant tries to calculate the right spot to be in. You want to be far enough back to let others soak up the oil, but close enough that someone else does not beat you to the money. After all of the maneuvering, you realize it does not matter, because none of the participants ever make it to the top in the first round.

After the first round, the ones who do not make it very far up the trunk are tossed out of the contest, leaving a smaller core of expert climbers. I was always tossed out in the first round, lacking the climbing skill or strength to compete with the "professionals." After each round more people are eliminated, until only a handful are vying for the prize at the end. These greased pole climbing pros know every trick in the book, like putting sand in their pockets, rubbing dirt on their clothes and hands, and wearing rough fabrics. You had to really want the $50, and many a kid ruined a pair of $20 blue jeans in a vain attempt to win the money. Inevitably a tall, skinny kid who had strong arms and legs won the prize. I was hopelessly outclassed.

Another favorite contest to watch was the tobacco spitting contest. Being good Church of Christ kids, there was no way we could be seen touching a tobacco product, so we were forever doomed to participate in the much less prestigious watermelon seed spitting contest. Nevertheless, we enjoyed rooting for our friends who engaged in the more messy spitting rivalries. This contest was a big affair, and a real crowd pleaser. Although the real pros were the men, some of whom could violently eject a huge cloud of spit for incredible distances, the real crowd-pleaser was the women's competition. We were fortunate that our more rural end of the county was blessed with an overabundance of girls who had no qualms about popping in a big plug and letting it fly in front of the crowds. We cheered them on with gusto, as we rode the school bus with many of them. The eager tobacco company representatives had no qualms in those days about giving free pouches of Red Man to anyone who was willing to participate, male or female, and age was no barrier to their generosity.

To set up the competition, the tobacco company representatives first distributed the chew. Box after box was opened, and when every contestant had at least one or two free pouches, more boxes were opened and hundreds of samples were thrown into the crowd. A thick sheet of white plastic with feet and inch marks was rolled out, and the contestants lined up. Chewing until they had saved up a large amount of spit, the challengers took turns letting it fly. Arching their backs, they then thrust their heads forward, ejecting the ample brown spit onto the white plastic, then wiping the drool off of their chin with the sleeves of their shirts. To be counted, the farthest "droplet" to be measured had to be at least as big as a dime in diameter. After the effort was measured and marked, a squeegee was used to clean the sheet for the next participant. The crowd, whipped into a frenzy by the free-flowing distribution of complimentary product, cheered each contestant on with enthusiasm.

Our family did not spend the night on the fairgrounds, but traveled to and from the event each day. This meant that we missed a lot of the "good stuff" that happened late at night, and which occupied the gossip mills the next morning. Rumors of late night romantic interludes among the kids who slept in campers, barns, and covered trucks for the week were rampant. Not surprisingly, most of the girls who were whispered to be involved in these events were also participants in the tobacco-spitting contest.

One year a girl we knew ended up running away from home with one of the migrant carnival workers. This was a big scandal in our neighborhood, as this was the kind of thing you might see on TV, but normally did not involve someone that you knew personally. I can still remember the guy; he ran the same ride every night, in which a series of "cars" rolled in a circle around a track that rose up and down at high rates of speed. The ride was characterized by loud, in-your-face rock music. The amazing thing about this "carnie" was that he played the same song over and over and over again; "Tush", by ZZ Top. He must have had it looped onto a cassette or 8-track tape, and we heard that song hundreds of times while roaming the carnival grounds night after night. This was in my mind a serious symptom of poor carnival management. I liked ZZ Top also, and it was a nice diversion from the country music that permeated every other aspect of the fair, but enough is enough. I guess it was his way of "announcing" that he, as the song said, "ain't asking for much, I'm just looking for some tush." Sure enough, by the end of the week he had found some.

The presence of these types of scandals is probably one of the reasons why our family slept in our own beds at home each night, thank you very much. Besides, my parents never were the camping out type. Each morning, we would pile into the back of my dad's truck, which still had the cattle racks installed for transporting our steers, and we would take the 30 minute ride to the Butcher Bend fairgrounds in the open air. On a few occasions we nearly froze to death, but usually it was warm enough in the July mornings to stand up in the back of the truck and let the wind whip into our faces as my dad drove down the highway. This was a blast, and we thoroughly enjoyed it all, except for the few times when we managed to get bugs in our mouths at a high rate of speed.

All in all, the fair was a wonderful place to spend a lazy summer week. Here, friendships were forged, summer romances bloomed then withered, and we learned a lot about life. It was time well spent.

Digging Fencepost Holes

If we wanted to make some spending money but were not old enough to drive, the options in rural Wood County were quite limited. The older boys would sometimes get lucky, landing a job at a sawmill or on a construction crew. But for most of us there was only one option, working on local farms. This did not come in the form of steady, dependable income, but was sporadic at best. You worked like mad when hay season was in, and hoped for occasional jobs doing other farm-oriented work in between.

In the mid 1970's, the going rate for most of us was around one dollar per hour. If we were lucky, we got $1.50 per hour. Once or twice I even made up to $2.50 per hour, but that was extremely rare, and involved working on some of the farms near Lubeck when their "teenage labor market" was tight. If I remember correctly, my "top" total summer take when working on farms was in the range of $400 or so. I thought I was in heaven. Most of that money was wasted on vinyl rock albums and cassette tapes, or blown on rides and rigged games at the county fair. I had no idea then that I should have been plowing it into Microsoft or Wal Mart stock. As is the case with most teenage boys, money has a tendency to burn a hole in your pocket, and the presence of any amount of cash causes uncontrollable urges that can only be relieved through capitalistic ventures.

In some cases, I was pressed into working for as little as 50 cents per hour. That was our problem—we had no bargaining power. First of all, there was no such thing as the "Early Teen Farm Workers and Pipe Fitters Local Union 307". Secondly, it was a buyer's market; the farmers generally had no problem finding labor willing to work for any wage. That was not just because we were hard up for work, but they learned the secret of obtaining labor without negotiation; asking the parents. I wish I had 50 cents for each time that my dad had "volunteered" me to work my tail off for poverty wages without asking me first. Once you were committed to go, it was too late to bargain over remuneration. Unfortunately, the federal government seemed to have no interest in enforcing the minimum wage laws on Hopewell Hill.

The master at tapping into the cheap labor market was Herman Hoffman. Herman's going rate was 50 cents per hour even after most farmers were paying $1.50 or more. He would pull us boys aside, apologize that he could not afford more, and then give us our assignments. While we were glad to get the 50 cents, we routinely complained under our breath and wondered why we ended up doing work for such low pay when we could be fishing or enjoying some other activities. Nonetheless, we did the work. Daniel Camp and I spent countless hours in his barn, wading in cow manure at least a foot thick, loading it into his spreader with pitchforks. While that was grueling, the hardest work of all was digging fencepost holes by hand.

Digging fencepost holes is a category of work all by itself. Many farmers used powered augers on tractors to dig the holes. Today, the technology has advanced, and they use a tractor driven "pile driver" to pound pressure-treated wood posts directly into the ground. After pounding for a few minutes the post is finished, and you can move on to the next one—you don't even have to fill in the dirt around the posts when you are done.

While Herman had a power auger, we routinely installed barded wire fence along steep, rocky slopes or in the woods where getting a tractor in place was not an option. So we were forced to dig the holes by hand, using the two-handled posthole diggers. Gripping both handles, you spread them apart, and then lift the digger up and down into the soil. Then you push the handles together, causing a clump of dirt to be gripped in the metal jaws. Then you pull the digger up and out of the hole, opening the handles to remove the dirt from the jaws. Basically, you repeat these steps over and over until you have a hole about two feet deep in the ground.

While it sounds easy, it is actually quite difficult. First, it can take anywhere from 50–100 "drive-downs" to dig a posthole, even when the soil conditions are perfect. Which, of course, was hardly ever the case. Quite often, you would run into thick clay or mud, and the dirt would not fall out of the jaws, but had to be scraped off with your boot or the jaws had to be pounded onto the ground to loosen the soil. More likely, we would run into good West Virginia shale or sandstone, and the posthole digger had to be exchanged for a "spud bar." A spud bar is a round rod, with a thick "blade" at one end that is used to drive into and bust up rock. At the other end is a larger diameter cap, used to pound the dirt back into the hole around the post after it is inserted into the hole. A typical spud bar weighs 8–10 pounds, which does not sound like much until you realize you will have to lift it up and drive it down forcibly thousands of times in a single day. So, you take the spud bar, use the blade to bust up a few inches of rock, trade it for the post-hole digger, remove the rock from the hole, and repeat this every few inches.

In rocky soil, the going is very slow and tedious. The first time out your arm muscles feel like Jell-O after the first hour, and when you realize that it is only 9 a.m., all hope is lost. Soreness and exhaustion sets in, making the going even slower. Each downward thrust becomes weaker and weaker, exacerbating the process. As sweat drips off your arms and head, the handles become slippery, and it becomes hard to get good leverage on the handles. When you finally get a hole completed, you drop in the post. The wood of choice for this is locust, as it is readily available in West Virginia, and it is almost impervious to rotting. A good locust fence post will last 25 years or more. You then have to pound the dirt back into the hole, a process known as "tamping". You kick in a few inches of dirt, pound it down with the dull end of the spud bar, and repeat the process until the pole is firmly seated into the ground.

The fun part of the job was putting the wire on the posts when you had a line finished. The barbed wire comes in round rolls. Running a rod through the middle of the roll, you attach this to a large U-shaped handle, and then pull the roll along the ground to unroll a single strand. Putting up barbed wire fence requires a few critical tools: a pair of pliers for cutting and twisting the wire, a "fence stretcher," leather gloves, a hammer, a leather tool belt, plenty of staples, and preferably a long-sleeved shirt and thick jeans. Pounding a staple firmly behind a barb on the first pole to keep the wire from slipping, you roll out a strand of wire, and then stop several fence posts down. Usually we made marks on the handle of the stretcher to gage how high each strand should be above the ground, so we would end up with consistent spacing between the wires.

The "fence stretcher" is the only real specialty tool that is required, although a real farmer always uses a set of pliers made just for installing fence. The fence stretcher consists of a handle, about 3 feet long, with a cleated metal "comb" at one end designed to "bite into" the wooden posts. It also has a short length of chain attached, with a set of "jaws" at the end that bite into a strand of wire when it is put into tension. You start by placing the metal comb on the fencepost. Then, gripping the wire in the "jaws", you stretch the wire tight across a post by pulling the handle. The trick is to start with the right amount of "slack" in the wire so that the angle is right when pulling on the handle. Then, using your legs to keep the handle tight, you pound a staple around the wire (preferably next to a barb, to prevent the wire from slipping) to keep it tight. If you can get a good pull on the handle, you can stretch out tightly as much as 50 to 75 feet of wire. Then you go back to all the posts in between, pounding in more staples until the wire is firmly attached to each post. When you finish the bottom row, you go back and put another strand up a foot or so higher. Usually four strands would work, but five was considered best.

Unfortunately, the fun work of putting up the wire went quickly. The real work was in digging the holes, dragging the fence posts from somewhere (usually the bottom of the hill) and tamping in the dirt. A day of this work usually left one dead tired, sore, and if not careful, dehydrated. And we did it all for the princely fee of 50 cents an hour. But after doing this for several days, we were in great shape, and could beat most of our friends in arm wrestling. And in our own peculiar way we enjoyed this work, in the solitude of the hills, with Herman's jovial manner and interesting tales making the day go by faster.

Several years ago Herman developed cancer. I saw him at church one Sunday morning, just a few months before he died. Pulling me aside after the services, his conversation quickly moved into an apology. "Brian," he said. "I was thinking about you the other day. I want to apologize to you for all of those hours I made you build fence and only paid you 50 cents an hour. What I did to you boys just wasn't right."

As I listened to his apology, I realized that this was one of the things that Herman was doing to prepare for his death, which he knew was not far away. But in my mind, he did not owe me an apology. I had never held a grudge or even thought much about it since then. But he was feeling guilt, and as he spoke, I realized that the time I had spent working on his farm had been time well spent. So I told him the truth.

"Herman," I said, "You have no need to apologize to me. You took a couple of boys under your wings, and helped make us into men. If I could do it all over again, I'd do it for free." With that, a big smile spread over his face, and he thanked me, shook my hand, and went on his way out of the building. I never had a chance to speak to him again. But I meant what I said with every fiber of my being. I wish for one day that I could go back into those hills with Herman, working hard, sharing a cup of cold spring water, and listening to his stories and anecdotes about his family and friends. I'd gladly pay for the opportunity.

Sunset on Bloomer's Knob

William and Margaret Bloomer (my mother's aunt) owned the second highest hill in Wood County. This rounded, dome-like hill was just across route 68 from our house. For us kids, it was the perfect place for kite flying, sledding, and quiet bouts of thoughtful dreaming. This hill that rises majestically above the hills and valleys of Hopewell is called Bloomer's knob.

During the summer months, we hiked to the top of the hill. Deceptively steep, the walk to the top will wind all but the most physically fit. What I loved was the view. From the high vantage point, one could see for miles. I spent many a moment mesmerized, watching the peaks and valleys of the West Virginia hills rise in pattern for miles until they melted into the horizon.

Bloomer's knob was also a great place at night, to lie on your back and watch for falling stars, or try to count how many radio antennas would cast their flashing red beacons into the darkness of the summer sky.

By far my favorite time to hike up Bloomer's knob was at sunset. Nestling into the tall grass, we would take our binoculars and prepare for nature's display to begin. For starters, as the sun began to settle, we tried to count the smokestacks from power plants miles away. They became very visible in the dusk as they spewed their clouds of steam and smoke across the darkening horizon. And, we continued to watch the sun lazily move down toward the edge of the earth, for from our tall vantage point, the curvature of our world became very apparent. We loved to watch the contrails formed by high-flying jets move progressively from sharp lines scratched into the window of the sky to dulled and blurred chalk lines, drifting in the upper currents until dissolving away.

As the sun sank low, the sky would begin to change colors, the blues and whites of the day yielding to yellows, oranges and reds, each shade darker as it approached the horizon. The colors across the canvas of the sky were mixed by wisps of cirrus clouds, as if the work of an impressionist Master. Meanwhile, the cumulus clouds would angrily darken at the top, while becoming brilliantly lit from underneath and within as though surrounding an incredible firestorm.

As the orb touched the horizon it seemed to speed up, as if it were anxious to be done with the day, ready to settle in for a long night's rest. We would watch this red sphere of fire as it dipped low, losing ground to the Earth as if the weight of Night's hand on its shoulder accelerated its demise. We would count the seconds until at last, the last thin sliver of the red inferno dipped out of sight, and the hills locked the sun in the prison of darkness.

Each sunset was different, depending on the pattern of cloud coverings and nature's mood. We never tired of God's handiwork, as each show recaptured our imagination through endless permutations, while renewing our awe of His marvelous handiwork.

Today, some 30 years later, the view from Bloomer's Knob is much the same, other than a few new houses or antennas. For change comes very slowly to Hopewell Hill, but that's the way those of us who call this area home prefer it to be.

Sassafras Tea

In the fall, after the leaves have fallen and the sap has returned to the roots of the trees, we looked forward to making sassafras tea.

The sassafras tree does not get very large, standing from 20 to 40 feet high, with many slender branches, and smooth, orange-brown bark. Sassafras has three types of leaves on the same tree, making it easily identifiable to the novice. The most common leaf has three distinct lobes, or "fingers", which all point away from the stem. The second type of leaf is the "mitten", which has one large lobe pointing away from the stem and a smaller side lobe that sticks out like a thumb. The third leaf is egg shaped with no lobes. I found that these leaves, along with locust leaves, were the favorites of our rabbits, who attacked them with gusto when I picked them and put them in their cages. These trees can live for over 800 years.

The leaves were off in the fall, as we trudged into the woods with our mattock and canvas bag to collect roots, but the trees were still easily identifiable by their unique bark as well as the size and shapes of the limbs. The bark of tree gives a slightly bitter, pungent taste, but the roots yield a most wonderful aromatic oil that provides for an excellent tea. The roots are large, soft and spongy, with a rough "bark" exterior, and are reddish or grayish-brown in color. Fortunately, the roots lie close to the ground, making them easy to harvest. We were always careful to take a limited amount of root from any single source—we did not want to kill the trees.

The sassafras smell is very unique, but difficult to describe. If you have never smelled sassafras, the closest thing to it is probably root beer. In fact, sassafras is a key ingredient in root beer, along with yeast, sugar, and usually ginger. Of course, people who make their own root beer "from scratch" usually have their own unique secret ingredients, like juniper berries, wintergreen, cinnamon, orange peel, vanilla, lemon juice, raspberries, or even dandelion root. In earlier times, sassafras was a key ingredient in every medicine cabinet, often used medicinally as a stimulant, diaphoretic (producing perspiration), and diuretic.

Our Mountaineer version of sassafras tea was much simpler. We simply cleaned the roots, chopped them into pieces, and put a handful (either fresh or dried) into a pot, and brought it to a boil. While still hot, we poured it into cups, mixed in enough sugar to make it sweet, and usually added a spoonful of milk to perfect the recipe.

Today many people use sassafras flavoring or artificially created sassafras oil for teas, root beer, or other recipes. I feel sorry for them, because they have been robbed of the real enjoyment and mystery of digging up the roots, the smell coming out of the ground and permeating the air as you work in anticipation of future reward. As is usually the case in life, substitutes are less expensive and less work, but they are less fun, not as educational, and I would argue, not as satisfying. There's nothing like the real deal.

Fireplace Memories

Unfortunately, my father did not discover the thermostat until after I was grown and had left the nest. Today, a newly installed central air system provides for my parents a cool, comfortable climate during the sticky summer months. This is a major improvement over the attic fan, which was never enough cooling when you went to bed, and too much cooling in the middle of the night. Also, my dad has supplemented his gas furnace with a wood burning furnace, and together they give out enough heat to make their house fit for a Saudi prince during the coldest winter snowstorms. However, when we were small children, electricity was seemingly as precious as gold, and you could almost see your breath in the house during the cold winter months.

Fortunately for us, Dad would light the fireplace when it got colder. It was a big moment for us, and we would watch with great anticipation as he carefully prepared the perfect fire. He would start with an absolutely clean fireplace, removing all of the ashes with his beloved fireplace shovel, and then brushing any dust off the hearth with a small whiskbroom. He would put down small kindling first upon the grate, followed by some crumpled newsprint, more kindling, ripped pieces of cardboard, and then more kindling, all tucked carefully together to give maximum lighting power (less time has been spent by many of the grand masters in creating their signature paintings...). Then he would carefully light the bottom layer of newsprint with a match.

When the fire started going pretty good, he would inevitably realize that he forgot to open the flue, and he would lunge toward the fireplace, battling through smoke and flames like a valiant fireman rescuing a soul in danger. Forgetting to open the flue is one of the two rules of life that apply to my dad; the other is that he always forgets to wind his 35 mm camera (he is always pushing down on the button and missing the perfect shot). When the smoke cleared and the fire was burning pretty good, he would add larger and larger pieces until he could add a huge log or two. The sparks would fly, and it would look like fireworks at the 4th of July! The whole living room would glow in oranges, reds and yellows, and we'd gather around the open fire for warmth.

After taking baths, we would sometimes go out by the fireplace to warm ourselves and to dry our hair. It felt so wonderful to stand there after a bath, wrapped in towels, the fireplace providing our only protection against the cold air. Mom would dress us right there, as we stood on the fireplace rug, trying to keep our bare feet off of the cold hardwood floor. Cold winter Sunday afternoons were also spent by the fireplace. Dad and Mom would rest and read the Sunday paper while my sister Leslie and I would play nearby. We would sit at our small wooden table and chairs, drawing and coloring while watching Mutual of Omaha's "Wild Kingdom" on television.

Now that was a great television show. We loved to watch it, but we always felt sorry for Jim, the loyal assistant to Marlin Perkins. "I'll stay in the Jeep while Jim wrestles with the alligator. Look out Jim! Those teeth are sharp!" It seemed that every episode they strained to work in a pitch for the Insurance, like when Marlin Perkins would interrupt the film to say something like this-"this hyena is getting torn apart by the pride of lions. You too can show your pride by investing in Mutual of Omaha's life assurance plan!" I used to hope that a poisonous snake would bite Jim or Marlin, so then we could find out how good that Mutual of Omaha insurance policy really was.

It is always a highlight to cook food in the fireplace. Mom made the best baked potatoes I ever tasted in that fireplace! She would carefully grease each potato after washing them and would wrap them in aluminum foil and then place them in the red-hot coals of the fireplace to bake. Those were REAL baked potatoes! I can still smell them as she would unwrap them and mash them with butter oozing over the edges. They tasted so good! We would roast hot dogs in the fireplace occasionally, too, on wire hanger sticks. Mom would use the coffee table as a picnic table, placing a cloth down on it and bring the mustard, ketchup, plates, cups, buns, onions and whatever else we had with supper there. We would have our own living room cookout, and then we would have roasted marshmallows for dessert.

When one of us got sick with the "croup", Mom would warm up a big towel on the hearth. She would get the towel very warm and would put it on our chest after greasing us down with Vicks Salve, rubbing it on our chests and under our noses. It usually worked to stop the coughing so we could finally go to sleep. That warmed towel felt so good when crawling in between the cold sheets in our bedrooms.

Although we enjoyed the fireplace, Mom got tired of all the wood being carried in and placed on the hearth. She would constantly pick up little chips and sticks off the floor and would have to run the sweeper just about every day in her never ending battle to keep it cleaned up.

By necessity, our living room was the center of activity in the winter months, as we could stay close to the fire. Leslie and I would come home from school, and then play cowboys and Indians under the coffee table in front of the fireplace. We would set up forts and play there for hours on end. With no VCR's, computers, DVD's or even record players, we were "forced" to use our imaginations when at play. We thought up a lot of our activities, as we didn't have too many toys when growing up.

Today, I am lucky enough to have a real wood-burning fireplace in my house. Although my hectic "grown-up" schedule does not allow much time for cutting firewood, I still have a load or two delivered each year. And just like when I was young, my family today sits around the fireplace on cold winter weekends, watching TV, reading, and cooking hot dogs, marshmallow smores and occasionally even "campfire pies". And it brings back childhood memories of those happy, simple times on Hopewell Hill.

If you have a fireplace in your home, but don't burn it, let me make a suggestion. Buy a small bundle of firewood or two, turn off the television, and gather your family around the fireplace as you light the fire. Pull out a board game, or perhaps some good books, and enjoy an evening together. You'll be glad you did.

Cutting Firewood

During the winter months, there were three words I dreaded to hear, "We need firewood." Firewood cutting was man's work, which meant it was up to my dad and I to embark into the winter cold on an expedition to bring home enough wood to keep the home fires burning. Unfortunately, this was usually a weekly event, taking up either Saturday morning or afternoon, and sometimes both.

The farmers sometimes even worked together to bring in the wood for winter. On one such occasion, when the old farmer Earl Kaufman was failing in health, about 20 of us gathered and worked for a whole day to stock up the winter's supply of wood for him. It was fun, cutting the trees, dragging them with tractors, piling the brush into big burning piles. The men used a tractor-powered cutoff saw to cut the limbs to length, its three-foot diameter blade singing effortlessly through the wood while violating every known OSHA workplace safety regulation. It was on this occasion that Burl Balderson nearly met his Maker, as he was dragging a large tree toward Earl's house with his tractor. I can see it in my mind as clear as if it were yesterday, the trunk of the tree digging into the ground, the long chain stretching and then snapping and sailing forcefully through the air, missing Burl's head and cowboy hat by what seemed to be a few mere inches.

I was convinced that cutting firewood was not a bad task if you did it correctly. The only problem was, we did it the wrong way. Most farmers thought about firewood in the spring, felling a stand of trees, and allowing them to dry in the summer heat for an abundant supply of winter fuel. The ones who were really on the ball went the next step, and had the wood dried, cut and stacked in the comfortable weather of autumn, before the first snowflake dared to fall from the sky.

My dad's technique, on the other hand, was to find and cut on Saturday just enough wood to maybe get us through the week. Had he been a businessman, his JIT (Just In Time) manufacturing method would have been ahead of his time. Although I had not yet achieved my engineering degree, or made it through middle school for that matter, I nonetheless knew enough about this JIT method to realize that it left a lot to be desired.

The other problem was that his method severely limited the flexibility of which trees we could cut. Rather than playing the roles of firewood hunters, conquering a particular stand of trees in it's entirety, we were the equivalent of firewood scavengers, forced to scour the woods like buzzards with chainsaws for the occasional dead and dry trees that were suitable for immediate combustion.

I quickly developed two laws of firewood cutting that seemed to apply without fail. One, the weather was sure to be terrible every Saturday afternoon. It was not unusual to find us cutting wood in the cold rain or blinding snow. And two, the dead and dry trees were always on the downhill side of the road.

The second point was important, because I was the designated firewood "hauler." My dad got to do the fun stuff, running the chainsaw, felling the trees and cutting them to length. I, on the other hand, was delegated to hauling the firewood to the truck. Cutting on the uphill side was always a treat, as you could roll the large pieces downhill to the road, or even give them a good heave and let them slide down a steep bank toward the truck. Unfortunately, this seemed to happen only on rare occasions, and I usually found myself trodding uphill, carrying endless armloads of wood through snow, mud and leaves. It was not unlike a movie they showed us at school, where carpenter ants would walk in endless circles around the edge of a plate, engaged in a macabre march to the death in a futile search for food.

In retrospect, this dreaded chore left indelible marks. To me the chainsaw was a remarkable instrument, and my dad played this instrument like a gifted artist. My dad used a red Homelite saw, with a 16-

inch bar and metal body construction. Unlike today's automatic oiling saws, his required constant attention to lubrication, and my dad's thumb was constantly pumping the oiler to keep the chain sliding freely. I loved the smell of it all, the oil, smoke, and hot metal intermixed with the savor of the freshly cut wood. My dad was meticulous on maintenance, lovingly brushing the sawdust off the saw with a paintbrush before removing the gas cap, wiping it down after oiling, and sharpening the teeth with his hand file between every tank of gas. He kept his oil, tools, rags and spare parts in a square milk crate, sized perfectly for the assortment of items he used, a practice I also follow to this day. When he bought a new saw several years ago, he stayed with Homelite, like the widower who can only bring himself to remarry a woman who is just like his first wife. He still keeps the old saw in running condition, and would no doubt be pleased to pull it out and coax it to life in a firewood emergency.

Every Saturday afternoon we were alone in our world, comfortable in our roles, running our weekly operation like a well-oiled machine. Occasionally my dad would allow me to take the saw and cut a piece of firewood, teaching me how to size up each cut, and showing me how to position myself to protect against backlash of the saw. It was here that he showed me to appreciate the simple things in life, like the way a perfectly sharpened blade chews into the wood, cutting a straight line and throwing out a stream of heavy sawdust in its wake.

Even more importantly, on some Saturdays he would emerge from the basement with two glass bottles of Coca Cola, carrying that precious cargo gingerly, as if was the nectar of the gods. As we headed into the woods and picked our cutting spot, he would drop the bottles into a snow bank or water spring. When the work was done, the truck was loaded, and the tools put away, he would give me a nod, and I would eagerly retrieve the bottles. Pulling a bottle opener from the crate, he would pop the top off each one, and we would sit on the tailgate and enjoy this rare treat in a silent celebration of manhood.

Today, we drink Coke like water, and the novelty of it has long ago worn off and become routine. But every once in a while, when I see a glass bottle, I think back to those snow-chilled treats, with ice crystals floating in the Coke behind the glass, and remember how the simple things in life can bring so much pleasure. Someday soon I hope my dad and I can grab two bottles of Coke, throw them into the snow, then pop the tops and enjoy them together after completing a few hours of hard work, maybe even splitting or cutting firewood. And we'll sit together, not saying much, just savoring one of the simple moments of life like we did many years ago.

Red

Every neighborhood has to have a "bully". It is one of those unwritten laws of nature in each generation of school kids; one bad seed must germinate and rise, towering over and dominating the other kids, as sure as ironweeds will take over any cow field that is not regularly mowed. The bully, like an ironweed, will establish himself at the top of the pecking order, dominating the rest of the neighborhood.

As kids, we never asked "why?" We just accepted, as Minister Phillips in his infinite wisdom might say, that God created people of all shapes, sizes, and dispositions. In our case, we ended up on the short end of the stick, at least in the shape and size department. We had to settle for disposition.

Another unwritten law of nature relating to bullies is that they have to have a nickname. No bully in his right mind has a formal name. After all, who would be afraid of someone with a name like Thomas Michael Rogers or Robert Franklin Davis? You might as well call Satan "Lucifer Percival Merriwether". No, only a nickname will do. Perhaps that is why to this day, I have no recollection of his first name. But his nickname was burned into my impressionable young memory long ago, "Red."

Red was the stockiest of four brothers, all part of the mysterious "Staats" clan who lived several miles down Pine Run Road. I knew where they lived, in a faded white farmhouse several miles from our bus stop. Occasionally we would drive by it when taking the back way somewhere, dust flying from the dirt as we scooted past. It was set back from the road, with toys, buckets, truck parts and sheet metal strewn in the weedy yard, surrounded by run-down sheds with drooping roofs, as though burdened by the weight of its mysterious secrets. I never saw any sign of life when we went past, and to this day I have never seen the Staats parents. For all we knew, Red and his brothers might not have been raised by their parents, but by mysterious foreigners who kidnapped them or perhaps even by creatures from outer space.

Red, in typical bully form, assaulted us not only verbally, but also physically, his every breath and action in some way a challenge to our existence. He even seemed to rule his older brothers, treating them in the same way. Day by day he pushed, prodded, teased, kicked, poked, stole, doing whatever he could to humiliate us and make our lives miserable. And it seemed he saved his best work for me, perhaps because of my short stature, skinny frame, and especially, I was convinced, because I wore glasses.

To this day, I cannot remember what action on his part became my "final straw". I only know that it happened. After years of being dominated and humiliated, my mind finally had enough. It was as if part of my brain had absorbed years of abuse and became completely saturated, and the pressure built up until I was ready to explode. An afternoon of teasing on the bus had somehow pushed me past the point of no return, and for the first time in my life I completely lost control. As this half of my brain took over, I dropped my books and ran full-tilt into Red and tackled him to the ground, the brute force of all 90 pounds of me driving him into the dirt and river gravel of Pine Run Road. This was, of course, a complete surprise to the other half of my brain, which could not believe my foolishness.

They say that dynamite comes in small packages. That was especially true of me on this spring afternoon, when my muscles miraculously mustered enough coordination to launch a full-force attack. In a crazed and wild frenzy, my fists began pummeling Red's face and chest as fast as they could. I was determined to get in every blow while I had the advantage of surprise. I lost track of what I was doing, as my vision tunneled and every fiber of my being coordinated itself into a furious attack.

Then, two amazing events took place.

First, Red began to cry. Tears streamed down through the dirt and dust on his face. Slowly, I came back to my senses, realizing that I had him utterly whipped. He was giving up all resistance; I was in complete control. I was shocked, and still convinced he would easily turn the tables and smash my face and glasses into a mangled mess. But he did not even manage a good lick.

Second, as my mind came back into focus, and my blows were slowing down, I saw my mother standing on the bank of the road, some 25 feet away, watching as I exhausted myself pummeling Red's body. I have no idea how long the fight had lasted to this point. I had lost all track of time in my dazed condition, but she had traveled at least 200 feet to get to her vantage point. I waited for her to rush in to stop the fight, but to my amazement, she held her ground. I am convinced that she secretly enjoyed seeing the tables turned on Red, knowing the terror he had wreaked on my sister Leslie and I. My mother was letting me drive the point home as long as no permanent physical damage was being inflicted.

Finally, I realized that the battle was over. I stood up, gathered my books, and quietly walked home. And although I was not carried off the field of battle on the shoulders of the other kids, I knew that I had gained for all of us some much needed respect, and that things fortunately would never be the same around the bus stop again.

Today, I realize that Red bullied us because of his own insecurities. He erected a wall of intolerance and bigotry to protect himself, but the wall had no substance, and when tested, it was amazing how easily it fell.

I also realized that inside each of us lies an amazing ability to focus our strength and will against an overwhelming foe. I sometimes think of this occasion when I feel overwhelmed by work or temptation, or burdened by the worries of the world. And I know that somehow I will gather my strength and face the foe head-on, winning an amazing victory.

I also gained a new appreciation for my mother that day. Some might say she was selfish or foolish to let me finish the fight. But, I think she deserved the chance to savor my unexpected victory. And secretly, in my heart, I believe I may have given her a gift on that mild spring afternoon far greater than anything I ever could have bought her.

Breaking the Whistler

I suppose that my generation is the last one that was able to enjoy the presence of "corporal punishment" at the hands of our public school servants. Today no teacher or administrator would dare lay a hand on any student, but in my time, paddlings were the preferred method of disciplinary action. No matter whether you are for or against spanking, you have to admit that it is, at least in the short term, effective. Some would argue that the effectiveness is counteracted by mental damage, but I have to admit I have never seen anyone with permanent psychological injuries from properly applied bodily punishment, as long as it was not excessive.

The second most common method of retribution, widely known for its amazing ineffectiveness, was banishing students to time off or study hall. I never understood why, in their infinite wisdom, principals would discipline someone who skipped school by sending them home for three days. It was the equivalent of forcing a hungry thief who stole food to visit an all-you-can-eat buffet. If only those administrators had an ounce of imagination, they could have come up with scores of more appropriate and effective punishments. For example, if someone skipped school, they could assign extra homework. Or, better yet, force them to sit in a room with Barry Manilow music playing nonstop. And instead of sending them into a loosely chaperoned study hall, where talking, spit wad battles and everything but studying was going on, I would have banished the evildoers to solitary confinement, or forced them to eat lunch in the teacher's lounge, although this would have caused permanent physical damage due to the secondhand smoke which rolled out in thick, gray clouds when the doors were opened.

I got an early introduction to the paddle in the first grade. Like most students in the late 1960's I did not go to kindergarten, so Mrs. McKissick's first grade class was my first exposure to organized schooling, outside of Bible class. I suppose I had a few things to learn about obeying orders. One day, while we were returning to our room from the gymnasium, Mrs. McKissick lined us up in two rows, told us to hold hands, and marched our column back to the classroom. Despite warning us not to run, the temptation in the front of the line was too great, and Barbara Cain and I broke into a fast trot, determined to be the first back to the room. It seemed like a relatively minor infraction to me, so we were surprised to find ourselves sitting outside the principal's office. Apparently Mrs. McKissick was having a bad day.

The first part of the punishment cycle was sitting outside the office. Like an inmate on death row, you were forced to slowly pass the time, thinking about what sort of torture was awaiting you on the other side of the big wooden door, which was closely guarded by the school secretary. Muffled classroom sounds emanated down the corridor, but they were not enough to drown out the ticking of the hallway clock, as the red second hand slowly wound its way around the face time and time again. Inevitably other students, clutching their hall passes tightly, would pass you on their way to perform some official errand. This added to your embarrassment as they gave you a smirk and rushed back to whisper to the others that you were in deep trouble.

After all of this, the spanking itself was almost a relief. Still, I was quite shocked, at the tender age of six, to find myself bending over to "assume the position" for no reason other than a short jog down the hallway. I suppose the blows were not all that hard, but after the contrived setup, the tightly controlled hallway wait, and the buildup of anticipation, it did not take much to break down the wall of resistance and leave you drowning in tears. I never ran down the hallway again. I was a new man, expressing real remorse and swearing off this early childhood brush with delinquency. This lasted until the seventh grade, when I was the recipient of not one, but two paddlings.

My first seventh grade miscue occurred outside, where my friends and I threw dirt into the air, watching the dust slowly travel across the playground. We did this despite repeated warnings from our administration, and paid the price for it on our backsides. I can still remember wondering if the force of the first blow would knock me forward, as I had very little leverage while holding my ankles. My second paddling that year was much more interesting. This one occurred in health class, which has held in one of the many "modular" buildings used to accommodate the overflowing attendance at Edison Junior High School. The teacher, Mr. Gaydac, had left the room for a while, and my friend J. E. Cochran and I were goofing off. We were pretending that we were fighting each other, throwing fake punches and landing make-believe blows to each other. As we were doing this, Mr. Gaydac walked suddenly back into the room, and was convinced we were really fighting each other. No amount of pleading could convince him otherwise. So, he marched us outside, forcing us to face the building while leaning forward with our hands on the wall. Then, he took out "The Whistler."

Like any good executioner, Mr. Gaydac took great pride in his instrument of death. In this case, it was a carefully crafted paddle, about three-quarters of an inch thick, with several rows of holes drilled through the paddle in an offset pattern. The holes, he took great joy in telling us, were to cut down on the wind resistance, making for maximum velocity potential as the paddle approached the rears of juvenile delinquents. I have no idea if that really made a difference, but for effect he would occasionally swing the Whistler through the air, and in our imaginations it seemed to break the sound barrier as it moved forward with a rapid "whoosh." When not employed, the Whistler occupied a place of honor on the wall of the classroom, an ever-present reminder of the price we would pay for stepping out of line.

Mr. Gaydac announced that I was to go first. I thought this to be extremely unfair, as Cochran came before Dowler, and the order of every other event on the cramped school campus was dictated by the alphabetical sequence of last names. (I had always felt sorry for Tim Zimm, who was relegated to the back of every classroom and went last at everything we did.) With great fanfare, Mr. Gaydac entered into his windup, and the Whistler shrieked through the air on its first pass, striking my backside forcibly. To my amazement, a loud crack rang through the air, and I realized that Mr. Gaydac had broken the Whistler on me! My first thought was relief, because I was, at least temporarily, spared from the rest of the planned series of blows. My second thought was anger, because I realized that my friend J. E. was about to get off scot-free. It wasn't fair! If possible, I would have glued the Whistler back together myself and endured several more blows, just to ensure that J. E. would get what he had coming to him.

It was unbelievable. The very holes drilled into the paddle to maximize velocity had weakened it enough to cause it to break into two when delivered with maximum force. To this day, I have no idea why the time-tested Whistler broke. Was Mr. Gaydac in an especially bad mood, swinging the paddle with more gusto than he had ever managed before? Or was I the beneficiary of a fatigue fracture, reaping the benefits of a tiny flaw that had, unbeknown to Mr. Gaydac, grown larger over the years on the buttocks of many students who predated me? Or did my wiry frame offer no padding to slow down the Whistler, causing it to snap like brittle glass? Whatever happened, I knew that this miracle had spared me a much harsher punishment, and I was extremely grateful.

Riding the School Bus

Riding on the school bus was somewhat scary for elementary students, as we were at the complete mercy of the middle and high school students. It was a virtual den of iniquity. Foul language, crude jokes, sexual tensions, unwanted groping, gambling, and other unsavory events were the order of the day. On several occasions, fights would break out, and we would dive for cover between the seats, gripping our metal lunch pails and Mead binders with white knuckles. On one such occasion, a student was poked in the face with a sharp pencil, which just missed his eye. Fortunately, I was usually able to seek a small shelter of protection via my older sister Leslie, who would sometimes jump to my defense if I got picked on unmercifully.

Even in elementary school, although living in a somewhat "protected" environment, we were used to occasional "country scraps" between kids. In the second grade, I got into such a fight with a classmate named Robert. It so happened that both of us were born on the same day, and thus had to "share" the special privileges normally given to whoever had a birthday in our class. Robert did not like that too much, and he decided to stab me with the weapon of choice in our circles, a sharp Pentel #2 pencil. I still carry the lead mark in my leg to this day. What a gift.

In the seventh grade, we rode the bus to Edison Junior High School, leaving the countryside and traveling some 15 miles into Parkersburg. I was already a veteran of the school bus environment, having survived six years of riding the bus to Lubeck Elementary with "George". George was an interesting driver. First of all, he had a harelip, and it took a few years to figure out what he was saying, as he mumbled his instructions to the largely un-listening audience of unruly students.

Secondly, he had the world's worst memory. On more than one occasion, he kicked me off of the bus, and told me not to ride again for a week. I just got on again the next day, like everyone else who got kicked off, and he would seemingly have no recollection of the previous day's events. In my later years, it was not unusual for us to ride three different buses each way, riding one bus to a school, making a transfer to another bus to go to a different school, and then sometimes repeating the process again. We made these carefully orchestrated changes like seasoned business travelers.

The big event to pass the time on the bus was "matching", a simple game of chance that we usually played with pennies, and if we were feeling big, nickels. If two people were playing, each person took a penny, pinched it between his index finger and thumb behind his back, then pulled it out, thumb up, with the thumb obscuring whether the penny was heads up or tails up. One person was the designated "match" winner, the other won all "no match" plays. The thumbs would lift up, and if both coins were either heads up or tails up, the "match" player received both pennies. If the coins did not match, the other person won. The fun was in trying to predict if the other person would play heads or tails, then you would try to adjust your coin for the win. As the odds were 50:50 either way, in general you could play for a long time without much of a difference in how many pennies you had. If we played all the way home on the bus and ended up 25 cents ahead, we considered it a good day.

The school bus was a constant in our lives. It ran in rain or shine, sleet or snow, and we could count on it to be there for us within minutes of the same schedule. In the winter, we would huddle up in the metal bus house, bundled against the cold, peeking through the bullet hole in the side of the shelter, until we saw the familiar yellow shape lumbering over the hill. Then, we'd scramble to the pickup spot, assume a single file line, and climb into the lively and noisy environment, happily beginning another day of our education.

Slingshots

No summer was complete without a new or refurbished slingshot. For all the boys on Hopewell Hill, the slingshot was our constant companion, and we could launch projectiles from them with remarkable accuracy forged by hour upon hour of practice.

My dad was a connoisseur of slingshots, and when in the woods his eyes were always glancing around as he looked for the "perfect split branch" to cut into a new one. The best slingshot sticks are from small trees, where a branch forms a symmetric split into two forked stems. I actually preferred one that was slightly non-symmetric; the stem that forked out at a steeper angle would be favored to the bottom, as my thumb rest. After cutting the branch down, the stems were cut to proper length, then stripped of all bark and the knots filed down until smooth. We then would carve a groove near the end of each of the two stems. The notches were made by carefully scribing two lines around the branches, about a fourth of an inch apart, then carving out the wood in between to a depth of about 1/8 inch.

Next came the tricky part; tying on the rubber tubing. While some of the boys used cut strips from inner tubes for the straps, we considered that second hand material, and dismissed them as rank amateurs. Rubber tubing was clearly a better material, and launched our rocks with more force and vigor. My dad had friends in the laboratory in the DuPont plant where he worked, and we never lacked for an abundant supply of the properly sized quarter inch rubber tubing. Taking one end of the tubing, we stretched it tightly around the groove in the sticks, and then tied it closed with strong string. We made knot after knot, wrapping the string around and around the tubing until we formed a tightly wound section that would not cut into the tubing.

Like tennis players with their racquets, we were constantly restringing our instruments, favoring the elongating properties of fresh rubber. With use and age, the rubber could become brittle, and when one breaks and snaps back toward your face, that can be really painful.

Next, we had to make the "pouch". The best pouch was thin, yet strong, and very flexible. We would make ours out of old leather gloves. A properly sized pouch is about an inch tall, and three inches long, with two holes cut close to each of the ends. We would measure out about 12 inches of tubing, then tie each end in the same manner as we used on the stems. Great care was taken to ensure that each strap was the same length. Then, after cutting the extra length off of the tubing, we were ready to rumble.

There is a big difference in how stones fly out of the slingshots. Flat stones whip out and curve off as they whip through the air, while smooth, round stones fly straight. Before heading out, we would scour the driveway for round stones, filling our pockets and cans before heading into the woods or to the dump to shoot cans and bottles. On a few rare occasions, we were lucky enough to get our hands on some old steel ball bearings, which were not just perfectly round, but very dense, making formidable projectiles. Around the fourth of July, we would put firecrackers in the pouch, let a friend light the fuse, and then shoot them into the sky. It's a wonder we still have all of our fingers.

There are different shooting techniques with slingshots. Most people, when they first start, hold the slingshot in their right hand and then stretch the pouch back toward their face, lining up the shot. While this is useful in visually lining up to the target, it has a real disadvantage in that the length you can stretch the tubing out is limited. Experienced "slingshotters" move quickly to the sidearm technique, where the open end of the stems is angled to the side, and the left arm pulls the pouch to the side. This enables you to achieve an incredible amount of stretch, and with enough practice, can provide just as much accuracy. Using this approach, we could launch a stone well over 100 yards away, and could launch rocks straight up into the sky, where they would go so high that we would lose sight of even a large stone.

With my homemade slingshots, I could routinely outdistance the high-dollar "professional" metal slingshots that some of my friends were buying at Sears. I think we appreciated our homemade slingshots even more. We took pride that we could fashion our slingshots with our own hands, making them work so well.

The Daisy and the Sparrow

Not long ago, my two sons, aged 12 and 14 at the time, saved up their money and purchased two BB guns at the local Wal Mart. My wife, a certified city girl, was horrified at the concept of our two boys shooting BB guns in suburban Camp Hill, Pennsylvania. For weeks, she suffered from cold sweats and nightmares, dreaming of young boys shooting out windows and eyeballs by accident.

I was much more nonchalant about the whole occasion, having spent many hours behind the sights of my own trusty Daisy BB gun as a young boy, albeit in a much more rural environment. I still have this gun, and it shoots BB's, but it has lost most of it's power, and the BB's exit the gun much too slowly, forcing you to aim well above the target, making a generous allowance for the effects of gravity, which is still as strong today as when the projectiles traveled at a much faster rate. So my sons, quickly tiring of my worn old gun, decided to splurge on new shiny guns, with multiple pump action and an optical scope above the barrel. Thus far no one has been injured, and I have not yet had to call in my umbrella liability policy.

I still find it hard to believe that I used to wander the woods carrying a .22 rifle as a young teenager. As I ran around shirtless and barefoot in the summertime, the gun and I forged a partnership, and I became quite a marksman for my age. My dad was a big fan of the .22 rifle, and taught me how to be careful with it, telling me how the bullets could carry for very long distance, and to always think about where the bullet might end up if I missed my target. During each fall hunting season, when my friends were knocking squirrels out of the trees with wide-range 12-gauge shotguns, my dad forced me to use the .22 rifle, as this was the more "sportsmanlike" thing to do. It may have been more sportsmanlike, but it was much more frustrating. While my friends were each stringing six squirrel tails on their car antennas the day after opening season, I would be lucky to have one. And in the world of budding manhood, having only one squirrel tail made one a second rate hunter, and my ego would inevitably suffer a blow for several weeks into the season.

During the summers, I made up for this by hunting crows. Crows are the disdain of every farmer, and my dad was more than glad to give me free rein to go after them with the rifle. Unlike squirrels, which tend to come out into shooting range if you sit still for a few minutes, crows are much more difficult to kill. They have much longer attention spans, and are smart enough to know if you are carrying a rifle. And once you mark yourself as the enemy, they are extremely cautious, and fly off into the distance if they know you are in the area. They work effectively as a team, and at the first "Caw" of the lookout crows, they fly off out of range. In all my years of hunting crows, I only managed to shoot one, and that was during one of my first crow hunting excursions. After that point, I was "marked" by the crows as a threat, and the crow clan never let me get close enough again to get off a good shot. And trying to hit a flying crow with a .22 rifle is next to impossible.

Before I roamed the hills with the .22 rifle, I had to cut my teeth on my beloved Daisy BB gun. I would practice for hours, shooting at tin cans, bottles, fence posts, tree trunks, rodents, or virtually anything that moved or stood still. Walking to the bottom of Pine Run Road, I would stand at the edge of the informal "dump", perfecting my marksmanship on cans and bottles. And although I often took potshots at chipmunks, squirrels and birds, I did not really expect to hit one.

Then, one day the odds caught up with me. Taking aim at a small wren on a nearby tree limb, I pulled off a shot, and much to my surprise the bird fluttered to the ground, completely dead. I ran over to the tree, and carefully picked up the small bird, confirming that it was dead. The warmth was still in its small, lifeless body, and a few drops of blood were the only sign of what had happened to it. Then, the reality of what I had just done hit me. I was not hunting for game, or even to eliminate a pest. Rather, I had indiscriminately killed an innocent animal for no good reason. Sadly, I placed the bird back on the ground and headed home, my appetite for shooting quelled by the event, and I resolved in my heart to never again kill an animal for no reason.

I do not feel that hunting or slaughtering animals for food is wrong, but I do believe that killing for no reason can be. And although I regret taking the life of the wren to this day, it was useful in teaching me a valuable lesson. It is easy to take things for granted. Just as I took the life of a small wren for granted, some people in this world can become so calloused as to take the life of other humans for granted. We can easily allow ourselves to be hardened to such actions, until we do not even feel the natural sadness and regret that should come when wasting a life that God has arranged. Sometimes today, when I find myself tempted to discount the value of someone's life, or to think of myself as more valuable to the world than another person, I remember the little wren, and resolve to honor the value of every life.

The Nimrod of Hopewell Hill

In the Book of Genesis, Nimrod is listed as a mighty hunter. But in the world of hunting I was strictly an amateur, never rising to the "professional" level of Nimrod, or even the other boys around the neighborhood. My friend Ronnie Breedlove and I would sometimes go hunting together, as we both fell into the rank of recreational huntsmen. While the other boys and men were well equipped with motor powered four wheelers, thermal camouflage suits, hand warmers, orange hunter vests and hats, hollow point ammunition and pre-defined hunting spots picked from their pre-season deer scouting excursions, Ronnie and I would stumble into the woods dressed in layers of unmatched clothing and no pre-determined plans.

If you play your cards right, you can legally kill several deer each year; a buck with a rifle, one with a bow, one with a muzzle loader, and sometimes they even hold special "doe seasons" in an attempt to reduce the burgeoning population. It is widely felt that there are more deer in West Virginia than people, and that was certainly true in our part of Wood County. It was not unusual to see a herd of 20 or 30 deer at a time, grazing together as they moved from the woods into the fields at dusk. But this abundance of deer seemed to suddenly disappear by hunting season, as the deer took cover in the underbrush. While most of my friends were concerned over how many deer they would kill each fall, I was still working on bagging my first one.

One year a mother deer had been critically injured in front of our house on Route 68, leaving behind a small fawn, only a few days old. This fawn was "adopted" by our neighbors, the Jim Phillips family, who gave it the creative name of "Bambi." Along with all the kids in the neighborhood, they raised the fawn, feeding it milk from bottles until it could eat grass, grain, and other solid foods. Bambi was incredibly tame, and hung around our houses, eating from our hands and playing with us. The deer grew rapidly, but when fall came, we all became very concerned about the fate of our now tame deer during hunting season. The doggone deer was so tame that it was likely to walk up behind an unsuspecting hunter and lick his ear. We all brainstormed ways to protect the deer, from locking it the barn or someone's garage to hauling it to the middle of a state park somewhere. Finally, Jim got a brilliant idea; he bought a can of fluorescent orange paint, and painted "PET" in huge letters on each side of Bambi on the day before deer season started. Surely, we thought, no one would shoot a bright orange deer. We congratulated him on this brilliant strategy, and felt sure we had finally hit on a plan that would work.

A few days later Bambi disappeared, and we never saw her again.

There are two basic deer hunting techniques that I was aware of. The first one was the "wait and let them come to you" approach, in which you sit silently along a path, waiting for the deer to walk by. This requires camouflage and patience, and is best done above ground level, in a tree stand. Tree stands come in many varieties, from the professional units that allow you to "walk" up the tree and back down, taking the stand with you, to homemade wooden varieties, with rungs nailed into the tree trunk providing access. Proficient deer hunters use other tricks, such as using scents or calls, and "baiting" the area in advance with corn or salt blocks.

Ronnie and I did not have any deer stands, and besides, we lacked much of the patience needed for the first technique. We usually chose the second one, "Drive the deer to you." This requires two or more people. It is as easy as it sounds; one person sits on a point or in a valley between hills, laying in waiting, while the others circle around and drive any deer out of the undergrowth toward the gunman. This was the method that Ronnie and I were using one Saturday morning. Quickly tiring of the "waiting" approach after an hour or two of unsuccessful hunting, we devised a plan. He sat on a hillside, while I circled around to drive any deer toward him. This proved to be unsuc-cessful, and we sat down on the wooded hillside, facing each other while talking loudly about the poor hunting conditions on the Bob Wigal farm. As we discussed the day's failure, a small and confused ant-lered buck came out of nowhere, and walked to a point in the trees about 30 feet behind Ronnie.

"Ronnie," I whispered. "Don't move. There's a deer behind you…"

"Get out," he said loudly. "Joker!"

"No really. There's a buck there," I whispered.

"No way!" he replied.

"OK," I said. "Then I'm going to take a shot."

As he laughed at my supposed practical joke, I lifted up my gun, and got off a shot as my heart pounded with excitement. It was an easy kill, as the .3030 rifle bullet made an effective entry just behind the front shoulder, and the deer dropped immediately to the ground.

Ronnie was bummed out. Being closer to the deer, he technically had "first rights" to the shot, but when he refused to believe the deer was there, I rightfully took it. We poked and prodded the deer to ensure it was really dead. We weren't sure how long it took a deer to die; most of our previous experience with dead deer was in incidences where they were struck senseless by cars on the highway. Then, we real-ized we had a dilemma. The deer was hundreds of feet from the nearest road or field. Even worse, neither one of us had ever gutted a deer before. It was not very cold, and we knew this was a crucial step to keep the meat fresh.

I decided to approach it just like skinning a rabbit or squirrel. I had seen my dad do this on countless occasions, and had used this experi-ence to learn how to do it myself. So, taking out my hunting knife, I tore into the deer with gusto. It was without a doubt one of the worst field dressing jobs in Hopewell history, but I somehow managed to get the job done. Leaving the remains behind for the foxes, we rolled, dragged and carried the deer carcass up the hill to my grandfather's

International Scout four-wheel drive. Hot, sweaty, and splattered with blood, we drove home to show off our conquest.

That single kill pretty much satisfied my hunting appetite, and I gave the sport up not long after. Having killed my first deer, I was now fully initiated into the good old boys club, my ego finally intact. And in a sacred rite of boyhood passage, I mounted the deer antlers to a wooden board that I had covered with green felt, making a tacky trophy of my great hunting prowess. This occupied a place of honor on my bedroom wall for several years, no doubt to the dismay of my mother.

The Hopewell Building

For our family, going to church was a simple affair, since our house was only 50 yards from the Hopewell Church of Christ building. We walked out of our front door, down the driveway, across the sidewalk in front of the cemetery and into the front door. Unfortunately, if we misbehaved badly during church, our parents could walk us out of the building, and then cut a "switch" from the tall poplar trees that lined our driveway. Or, worse yet, they would give us the knife and let us cut our own "switch." The anticipation was worse than the spanking in most cases.

The Hopewell building was a traditional "country" church building: wooden siding painted white, with a steeple and several windows down each side of the auditorium. Because wood was the most convenient building material in the early 1930's, the founding fathers had settled on a minimalistic architectural style, with wooden floors, pews, and pulpit. This, of course, fit well with the conservative approach favored by those church fathers. Over time the building had been updated somewhat, with a drop ceiling and fluorescent lighting, a small foyer and restrooms tacked onto the front entrance, a PA system, and an addition for classrooms in the back. But alas, no air conditioning. So in the late 60's and early 70's, this eclectic mix of architectural influences greeted those who entered.

The wooden floors were sloped slightly downward toward the pulpit. On more than one occasion, one of my friends would accidentally drop a coin, ball or marble from their pockets, resulting in a loud clank and a slow, agonizing roll all the way to the front of the auditorium. Once in a while other unwanted noises would disrupt the services, the most notable being when the PA system would pick up the CB radio signals from an 18-wheel truck passing by the building, and broadcast them plainly for all to hear for 15–30 seconds. Fortunately, the system never broadcast a trucker in the middle of a "course language" diatribe for which they are known.

The basement of the old Hopewell building was a somewhat scary place. Descending down old wooden steps through a narrow cement walkway, you emerged into a cellar-like room with a low ceiling that led into several classrooms. As you descended the steps, a strong musty scent permeated the air. This smell was, in my youthful imagination, the combination of mold, dead rodents, and water seeping into the basement from the graveyard. We kids spent countless hours discussing if the basement did, in fact, smell like dead bodies. The basement also had a scary crawlspace that went back under the auditorium. Occasionally, one of the men would have to go in there to perform some utility work, but you could not have paid me enough money to go in there. Mice inhabited the building in abundance, both in the basement and in the attic, and the men were constantly setting out traps and poison in an attempt to keep them under control.

As soon as services were over, us kids would rush outside to play in the churchyard. We were continually subject to admonitions from the church elders not to play in the cemetery; for there were always concerns that an old tombstone would fall over and kill one of us. Hence, we limited out exploits to the sidewalks and small lower yard. It was here that I learned how to play "Red Rover," a game in which we would take a long running start and try to break through a "line" of people who were tightly gripping arms together. I have no idea how we played all those years without someone breaking an arm! We also played games like "Simon Says" to keep ourselves entertained.

During the hot summer nights, the churchyard and graveyard were our frequent playgrounds. It did not seem like a scary place to us; we grew up right next to it, and spent countless hours playing among the old tombstones. We used to sit against the tombstones at night, warming our backs on the radiating granite as we watched the stars and discussed life. We would often play hide and seek in the graveyard, and knew our way around it so well that we could find the larger stones even in the dark. One overcast night, not knowing a funeral was scheduled the next day, I nearly fell into a freshly dug grave while playing in the dark. That was scary.

Another key pastime that centered around the old Hopewell building was trying to "catch" bats. The steeple was continually home to a colony of bats. Every night they would fly nonstop around the light pole in front of the building, feeding on the bugs attracted to the light. We used to fill our pockets with small stones, then head for the light pole with baseball bats, tennis rackets, nets, or anything else we thought might be useful in catching a bat. We would throw the rocks into the air, tricking the bats into thinking it was a large bug. The bats would dive down, following the rock, and sometimes chasing it all the way to the ground before figuring out it was a false alarm. As the bats came close to the ground, we would swing our bats and rackets at them, hoping to hit one. We never did, they were just to fast, and their reaction time incredibly fast. But it was the best game in town, and we entertained ourselves for hours on end, each "close call" lifting our spirits and invigorating our resolve. One night, a bat flew down and "brushed" my sister Leslie's long blonde hair. Thinking the bat was in her hair, she panicked, and started flailing around, rolling on the ground, and beating her hair like it was on fire. We never laughed so hard in all of our lives.

Several years ago, the building was torn down, and a new building erected at a different location with more room to expand. The ground was leveled, making room for more cemetery spots. A few years later, one of previous ministers, Joe Richards, passed away. He was buried in the very spot where the old pulpit stood. Also, the old concrete steps that led from the road up to the building were kept in place. These are the only two visible reminders of the grand old building that stood in place for many years, serving the people of the Hopewell community so well.

Reserved Seating

Humans are creatures of habit. During church services, my family always sat in the same pew, rain or shine, early or late, sick or well. Everyone knows, even to this day, that in the Hopewell Church of Christ building, the outside section of the third pew on the right side is reserved for the Dowler clan. If we showed up to church 10 minutes late, that spot was still guaranteed to be open. (Not that we would ever have committed such a deed, punishable by raised eyebrows and glances of consternation. Sitting in the front gave us more incentive to show up on time.) For all practical purposes, we could have carved our names in the pew, and personalized our space with pictures, knick-knacks, and a few small potted plants to make ourselves feel even more at home.

On one occasion, we entered the building to find that some visitors had occupied our beloved third-row abode, and in their unknowing ignorance now had squatter's rights to our claim. This, of course, caused a moment of quiet confusion in our family. This had never happened before. What would we do? Where would we sit? Should we politely inform them that we always sat in this location? Why had not any other church members steered them toward a section of seating not usually held in reserve? Eventually we recovered enough to slide into a seat several rows back as services were starting. And though we made it through the services fine, it just did not feel right, and we knew that people were watching us to see how we would react to this unexpected incident. It took several weeks in our normal spot until we felt fully back in the groove.

For many years, even after I had grown up and attended several different congregations, I routinely sat on the front right section out of habit. It still feels a little strange to me to sit on the left side, or toward the back of the auditorium. In my mind, it seemed that sitting in the front was a subtle way of signaling that you were a strong Christian, at the forefront of the congregation, willing to be seen by others. Although never said, it seemed implied that sitting toward the front was the "most perfect and excellent way." There are fewer distractions, the singing sounds better, you get a close up view of the speaker, and people are not crammed in so tightly like in the back rows, where they wedge into the pews as though their lives depend on making a quick getaway as soon as the last "amen" echoes off the building walls. I still have not figured out why, in every other event and venture, the front rows are coveted except for in church services. I used to fantasize that one day the preacher could walk to the back of the auditorium, drag in a portable podium, and force all those back row regulars to endure a service front and center. Alas, it never happened.

Shortly after the Hopewell congregation built a new building with much greater seating capacity, the church leaders roped off the back few rows to encourage members to move slightly toward the front of the building. The idea was to keep us from being so spread out. This, of course, was not well received. People literally tore the ropes off the pews and sat down in the back rows anyway, as if challenging the church elders to deny them their constitutional right to sit there. I am convinced that had they unscrewed the pews and removed them from the building, these members would have marched to the basement, secured folding chairs, and defiantly sat in the open space at the rear of the auditorium. Then, they would have hastily constructed pews out of plywood and scraps of wood they had lying around, dragging them into the auditorium before the next service to hungrily feed their back row addiction. Some things never change.

Gospel Meetings and Sings

Unfortunately, the gospel meeting is a dying event. In today's fast-paced world, with jobs demanding long hours, an abundance of youth sport activities, a profusion of alternative entertainment choices, and short attention spans, it has for the most part ceased to be an effective outreach tool for most churches. Most people will acknowledge that it is just too difficult to get people to attend these events today. But, there was a time when a gospel meeting was a real community event, well attended, and a real occasion to fill the pews with members and non-members alike. To be honest, I believe that these events hit their peak well before I was born in 1962, but they were still going strong in the late 60's and early 70's, when my impression of these events was forged.

A true gospel meeting is characterized by its length. We used to hear the "old timers" tell how in times past that people would come for miles around, attending a "big event" meeting every evening for two weeks or more. But most of the meetings that I attended were only weeklong events. A gospel meeting is also characterized by bringing in an outside speaker, preferably one with a reputation for being a dynamic speaker. They are routinely held twice a year, once in the spring, and once in the fall.

I vaguely remember attending a tent meeting held in Belleville West Virginia, in the Ohio River bottom. I must have been very young at the time, because I can only recall two scenes from this meeting. The first is just a mental picture of the large tent, filled with row after row of folding chairs, with light bulbs hanging from wires strung up above. The second image is of several men and boys walking to an abandoned church building nearby, chasing bats out of the structure by throwing rocks in the belfry.

While many people looked forward to these gospel meetings, they were for the most part an adult event. For a young boy, a meeting was an unwelcome diversion, something that took away precious play time each evening. And to make it worse, being featured in a gospel meeting seemed to give the speaker some sort of magical license to extend the sermon well beyond the normal and customary time allowance. Sermons of an hour or more were not uncommon. Combine this with a hot, stuffy building without air conditioning, and you have the perfect recipe for pre-teen boredom.

To make things bearable, we naturally had to create diversions. If we were really lucky, a mouse would run over the clear fluorescent light panels above our heads, giving us an amusing display of rodent behavior. But we normally had to settle for the usual diversions, such as folding papers, catching flies, or playing with the funeral home fans that people were desperately waving back and forth in a futile attempt to reach some semblance of personal comfort.

Usually Bob Emerick would sit in the second pew, one row in front of our normal position. Bob had thinning hair, and with the help of generous doses of oil, he combed a large swirl from the front over the top of his head, forming a sort of hollow spiraling section. As a young bored lad in these gospel meetings, I would instantly perk up whenever a fly started swarming around Bob, occasionally landing on his head. Holding my breath in baited anticipation, I would silently beg for the fly to walk into the oversized swirl, only to be caught inside this inadvertent insect cage, like in a Venus flytrap. Unfortunately, it never happened.

As I grew older, I came to appreciate these gospel meetings. Although I have forgotten the names of many of men who filled our pulpit, I can still remember many of the sermons. I particularly remember one meeting, where the speaker had painstakingly prepared large "charts" on white sheets. Each sheet was hung in place before the lesson, and a long wooden pointer was employed as the lesson was presented. I have to admit I was fascinated with the approach, and I got more out of these lessons than from any "PowerPoint sermon" I have seen since. I particularly remember one sheet, showing man's transition from earth to Heaven or Hell, with Paradise in between, and a host of supporting scriptures listed as reference. This was fascinating stuff to me at that juncture in my life, when I was coming to terms with my own mortality and spirituality.

Another variant of the gospel meeting, and a true heritage of the Churches of Christ, are the old time acapella "gospel sings". Usually, these rotated from congregation to congregation, and were very well attended from people all around the community. The normal routine is to ask all the men who were song leaders to come up front, and they take turns leading the songs. Each man picks out a few favorites, usually two, which they lead before giving the floor to the next man. Other than a few uncomfortable pauses, when no one knows exactly who is to go next, this system works pretty well. Seasoned song leading veterans know to pick out 3 or 4 songs, so they can adjust if someone before them picks out one of the ones they wanted to lead.

The other approach is to ask the congregation for requests, resulting in a rapid-fire burst of numbers that were captured on a blackboard. This invites audience participation, always a crowd pleaser, and those who are too embarrassed to shout out a number will invariably whisper something like "Say number 465! Say number 465!" to the person next to them. After the board is filled with an adequate number of selections, each song leader leads two of the songs on the board, his service highlighted by the opportunity to take the eraser and wipe off two of the numbers after he has finished.

Nothing sounds as good as a packed building, led by a great song leader, pulling their voices together in four part harmony on an old gospel classic hymn.

Of course, the singing was not always this good in the regular services. However, the Hopewell congregation takes singing seriously, and has always had strong singing in their worship. When I was young, we routinely had Wednesday night song practices, led under the watchful eye of one of our elders, Wilbert Hoffman. When it came to singing, Wilbert ruled with an iron fist. Or I should say, an iron foot. Whether leading, or sitting in the second row giving tutelage to the other leaders, his foot unfailingly tapped the beat of the songs we sung. If the song leader or members of the congregation "dragged" a song, or dared sing out of key, his foot tapping and his voice got louder and louder, until he again seized control of the song, dragging the song back from the edge of disaster into a respectable performance. With a strong voice, rhythmic foot, and trusty tuning fork, Wilbert whipped us into a lean, mean, singing machine in true military style. His legacy lives on today, in the form of strong and effective singing at the Hopewell congregation.

Hopewell Nazis

In our middle school years, my friends and I created a significant disturbance in the Hopewell congregation with our homemade comic books. Cutting normal sheets of plain paper in half, then folding them over into fourth-page booklets, we made these comic books using the meager materials we had on hand. A few staples along the spine ensured that they stayed together. We then would create our own comic books, filled with stupid, juvenile humor, often drawing rudimentary caricatures of people we knew in imaginary and often unflattering situations. Most of this humor was inspired by the "Mad" comic books, which we devoured anytime someone was able to get their hands on one. As most of the people that we knew were in our community, our comic strips were filled with characters from our church, and we would clandestinely pass them around during church as a diversion during long sermons.

Unfortunately for us, a few of these top-secret comics made it out of our clutches and into the hands of the adult members of the congregation, who were no doubt perturbed to see themselves parodied so ruthlessly. Although the books in and of themselves were quite harmless, they were in poor taste, and we should not have been passing them around in church. But what really got us in trouble were two specific items. First, each of the comic books was headed by the title "The Hopewell Gang." Second, with the "authors" not knowing the significance of what they were doing, or even what it really meant, a few of the comic books were illustrated with Nazi swastikas. At any rate, a few people "put two and two together" and decided that a Nazi skinhead gang must have stumbled out of L.A. and infiltrated the naïve, young, and fertile minds of the children of Hopewell, West Virginia.

Soon, the rumor mill was running rampant. One rumor said that we had a secret tree house in the woods, where we invited young children, engaged in their dark ritualistic events, and brainwashed them into the gang. According to another rumor, the Nazi propaganda was just a cover-up for the real hardcore satanic influences we were getting into. This was, of course, news to us, since we did not even have a tree house and never would have dreamed of dabbling in the occult. (Other than the one time a bunch of us messed around with an Ouiji board in our basement…)

We found the whole situation somewhat interesting. First, we were definitely not a "gang", and in all actuality did not realize the significance of the term at the time. Secondly, we barely knew what a "Nazi" was, other than what we had picked up from watching the bumbling Colonel Wilhelm Klink and Sergeant Hans Schultz on "Hogan's Heroes." We had no idea of the deep "political" implications of the swastika symbol at that early point in our lives, or what the "National-sozialistische deutsche Arbeiter-Partei" stood for. To be honest, I am pretty sure I had not even heard of the Holocaust at that point of my sheltered life. We just knew it pulled a few strings, and we ignorantly latched onto it as a misguided way of making our comic books as outrageous as possible.

Nevertheless, an "emergency" meeting of concerned parents was called and conducted in the basement of the parsonage, presided over by our minister Jim Phillips, who was also incidentally the parent of Joey, one of our partners in crime. Although the meeting was for adults only, we managed to peek in through the basement window, and we watched the unfolding of events for a while. When total boredom set in, we trudged back up to my house to find something more interesting to do. We were, however, quite concerned, not knowing what sort of "punishment" might be coming our way. We expected it to fall somewhere between a good lashing and being sequestered to a top-secret U.S. government de-brainwashing facility in the middle of the Utah desert.

Much to my surprise, when my parents came home after the meeting, instead of banishing me to my room for a month or whipping my hind side, they laughed the whole thing off, told me it was all blown out of proportion, advised me to lay off the cartoons for a while, explained to me the meaning of the swastika, and then went about their business like the whole thing had never even happened. In fact, I found out that most of the parents involved had taken the same view of the events, and had informed one set of overreacting parents who created the "controversy" to take a chill pill. I was blown away. Suddenly, I saw my parents in a whole new light, and gained a new appreciation of their reasoning abilities. They did not just blindly come down on me, both guns blazing, shooting first and asking questions later. They were able to see the whole thing for what it was—the ill-advised actions of a group of ignorant and bored pre-teen boys. And they did the right thing.

Looking back on the whole thing now, with an adult point of view, I of course realize that what we did was wrong. We should not have been passing around artwork in church, and we especially should not have invoked the swastika on our artwork to get a reaction. I can only claim ignorance in that regard, and today I try to raise my children not to be racist or prejudiced in any way. But, I also gained an understanding that if imaginations run unchecked, things can get blown out of proportion, and it's best to learn the facts before jumping to conclusions. It was a valuable life lesson, and I didn't grow up to be a skinhead after all.

Earl and Lena

Earl Kaufman was a giant among men. Not just in stature, although he was one of the tallest men around. But he was a spiritual giant, and a leader in our church and community. Earl knew the Bible inside out, and had an amazing ability to quote and recall passages on demand. As a young boy, I was awed at his ability to quote scripture, and realized that he had spent countless hours in the Word. My friends and I used to dread when it was his turn to pray at church; he normally took 15 minutes or more, and as kids we agonized through every word in the hot summer heat and humidity. It was only later in life that I gained an appreciation for his heartfelt prayers, and the knowledge and care of this elder in our church.

In the early years of the Hopewell Church of Christ, there were times when they depended on itinerant preachers. If one did not show up on a particular Sunday, Earl and the other church leaders would ask each other, "Do you want to preach today?" A typical response would be, "Well, I can, but do you want to do it?" This would go on for a while, until finally it was settled. On many occasions, Earl climbed to the old wooden pulpit, and preached a resounding sermon with no notes and on no notice. It was only later in life that I learned that this self-made man had a third grade formal education. This sort of spiritual capacity was not uncommon among the simple farming men of their era, for whom religion was their main pastime. They grew up well before the days of home electricity, without TV and other electronic diversions, and reading the Bible by lamplight was their primary evening activity.

Not long after their marriage, Earl and Lena acquired several hundred acres of West Virginia woodlands, and began the backbreaking task of turning it into a farm. I imagine Earl in those days as a tall, strapping man, and can picture him working from dawn to dusk, cutting trees by hand and hitching horses to haul trees and rocks out of the ground to carve out pastures. These were the days before power tools, and every acre was gained only through backbreaking labor. Barns were built, a two-story farmhouse constructed, and a hard life on the farm established. In addition to cattle, for many years they had a large turkey farm, until the success of large "super farms" made poultry farming difficult for independent farmers.

Lena was as short as Earl was tall, and seemingly spent most of her hours on two activities, cooking and weaving. Lena had a loom, which she kept in the living room of their house. This seemed like a magical instrument to us when we were children. From time to time, she would give a demonstration of how it worked. We would watch in wonderment as she sat on the wooden stool, tossing the spindle back and forth among the colorful strings lined up in parallel rows, the loom moving back and forth in singsong fashion. Although she could weave cloth, her "specialty" was using the loom to make rugs, and we would collect and tear strips of leftover cloth for her to weave into rugs.

I only knew Earl and his wife Lena in their later years, as they were probably already in their 60's when I was born. Even at that age, Earl was still strong as an ox, and he and Lena worked tirelessly on his farm along with his son Averill, my uncle. When on the farm, Earl was inevitably dressed in overalls with a cotton shirt, with an old cloth handkerchief stuffed in the front pocket. In his later years, Earl "graduated" primarily to tractor driver, thus leaving the heavier work to Averill and the boys they would hire to help them on the farm. Although Earl and Averill had separate adjoining farms, they constantly worked together, and were inseparable. We would be hired from time to time for different chores, but primarily for "putting in" hay. The pay was not great; most of us worked for $1.00 or $1.50 an hour, but on occasion we had to work for 50 or 75 cents an hour. There were side benefits, however; we had meals provided, and all the cold well water we could drink.

I vividly remember one such lunch break at Earl's farm. Lena had prepared an array of sandwiches, which we tore into with gusto. Averill began joking around, and started eating a piece of lettuce while pretending to be a rabbit. As he pushed the lettuce bit by bit, my friends and I noticed a small green worm crawling on the lettuce! Averill, of course, did not see the worm, and our laughter only spurred him on to keep the bunny routine going. He was no doubt pleased at the success of his gag, and had no idea why we were laughing so hard. As the worm edged closer and closer to his mouth, we were laughing too hard to tell Averill what was going on, and the worm finally made it into his mouth as he chomped down on the lettuce. We never did tell him what happened, and were sure to examine the rest of the lettuce very carefully while making our sandwiches.

In their later years, Earl and Lena were devastated by the death of Averill in a farming accident. They never really recovered from this tragic event, and now childless, they struggled to maintain their farming lifestyle on their own in declining health. Finally, they were forced to sell the farm and move into town. We watched in sorrow as their health declined, and these once proud and strong farmers, who forged hundreds of acres into a farm that sustained them for over 50 years, were forced to live their final days sharing a small room in a nursing home. It hardly seemed fair.

Ernie's Mighty Easter Egg Hunt

The coming of Easter signals the arrival of spring, a time when the ground shrugs off the snow and the weariness of winter, giving way to the daffodils who emerge after a long winter of hibernation. They burst from the ground, lifting their blooms above their thin and fragile stems like the weight of the world on the shoulders of Atlas. My mother is a prolific flower gardener, and as a child we spent many hours pouring over books like the Burpee Seed Company catalog, admiring the strains of flowers and plants that were available by mail. Each year we would place our order, then when the box arrived, we tore through cardboard and sawdust until reaching our precious cargo of bulbs—tulips, daffodils, hyacinths, bluebells, irises, crocuses, gladiolas, lilies and as a treat an occasional exotic plant, like a "jack in the pulpit." We would plant our stash carefully, like pirates hiding gold treasure in the sand, then wait for the spring rains to awake our dormant bulbs, bringing forth an amazing rainbow of colors that surrounded our home and brightened our days.

In the fall, we would dig up the mature beds, carefully separating the bulbs and storing them in sawdust until spring. I was always amazed at how the bulbs could dry out for the entire winter without dying, actually strengthened and toughened by this process so that they became hardier plants. In the early spring we would retrieve these bags of bulbs, planting them throughout the yard in anticipation of their flowery harvest.

Being members of the Church of Christ, we did not celebrate holidays in a "religious" manner. Rather, we heeded Paul's admonishment not to observe special times in Galatians 4:9–11, and as a collective body had practically memorized the King James translation of this passage: "But now, after that ye have known God, or rather are known of God, how turn ye again to the weak and beggarly elements, whereunto ye desire again to be in bondage? Ye observe days, and months, and times, and years. I am afraid of you, lest I have bestowed upon you labour in vain." Many a sermon was preached on this passage from our worn wooden pulpit, particularly in the weeks preceding Easter and Christmas.

Despite these admonitions, we still somehow managed to draw large crowds on Easter, mainly people who were not in the pews on the previous weeks when Paul's admonition was so eloquently expounded upon. I always thought this was the wrong strategy, kind of like spanking the kids who did not skip school and letting the ones who did skip come back to class the next day with no penalty or mention of their truancy. The same logic applied to sermons on "not forsaking the assembly," which always seemed to be delivered on Sunday evenings, when the ones who needed to hear it the most were not there to hear it. I always rooted for the preacher to ascend the steps to the pulpit, then rip loose a fire-breathing sermon on these same topics on Easter Sunday, like an old puritan hell fire and brimstone minister. But it never seemed to happen, and the Easter Sunday sermon always seemed to be aligned along gentler and less controversial lines of thought. Thus, attempting to not celebrate the holiday in a secular manner, we did not know whether to be glad or embarrassed to see so many people crowding the pews during holiday services.

As Easter approached, our attention quickly turned to eggs and candy. One of the highlights of the holiday was pulling out one of the Paar egg coloring kits, purchased for 79 cents at Ralph's Market during one of our Saturday expeditions to Parkersburg. As our mother boiled water on the stove, we would quickly set up 6 coffee cups, dropping a colored tablet into each. Then mom would pour in the water, dissolving the tablets, and we would drop boiled eggs into the cups with the gold-colored wire egg holder, carefully turning the eggs over to maintain an even coloration. After we did the first batch of eggs, we usually decided to get creative, writing on the eggs with a wax pencil to obtain white lined drawings after the eggs were dried, also mixing the colors and making eggs with each half a different color. After allowing the eggs to dry, we were ready for the family Easter egg hunt, which we traditionally did on Sunday morning before church.

One year, after a warm spring season, we were especially excited about the egg hunt. The grass had grown much taller than usual for this time of year, and was a good four inches tall, perfect for hiding the eggs. On Saturday, we were looking out the plate glass windows, excitedly thinking about the next day's hunt, when we saw my dad climbing onto his riding mower. We were horrified—who in his right mind would think about spoiling the perfect Easter opportunity? We did the only thing we knew to do, enlisting our mother in the cause. Together we made an impassioned plea to my dad, begging him to at least not mow the front yard.

Knowing he could not mow on Sunday, which was taboo back in those "blue law" days, dad was worried sick that the rain would come, and that by the time it dried out enough to mow, the grass would be so tall that it could not be cut. "Never fear," he told us, "I'll leave an unmowed patch for you to have your Easter egg hunt in." Confident that his word was his bond, we went back inside to play while he began cutting the grass.

Later, we stepped outside, and seeing the yard, our faces quickly dropped. Dad had left a patch of tall grass, smack dab in front of the front porch, but it was only about 3 feet in diameter! It seems my dad had been cutting the edges of the once large patch, and in an attempt to get a perfect circle he had lost control of the situation, ending up with the tiny patch of grass he was now presenting to us. Any multicelled life form would have been able to find every egg hidden in that small island of grass in three seconds or less. My mom came out of the front door, stood on the porch, hands on her hips, and muttered "Ernie!" in a deep tone, as she always did when she wanted to scold my dad. Then, turning around, she marched back into the house, screen door slamming behind her as if on cue to add a poignant explanation point to her brief but effective scolding. We were devastated.

The next morning, we had our Easter egg hunt after all. And though there were a few eggs in the tall patch, my parents got creative and used the flowerbeds and shrubbery to augment the number of hiding places, and we managed to have fun with it after all. When we went back inside after the hunt, we each found our customary cellophane-wrapped basket, full of "robin eggs", chocolate "footballs" and of course a hollow chocolate bunny, each guaranteed to lose its ears and candy eyes in the first part of the feeding frenzy. And who can forget those little yellow chick "peepers" made of yellow sugar coated marshmallows?

We will always remember the tiny patch of grass my dad left for us that year, and we still make sure we remind him of this from time to time, even though it is now decades after it happened. It is a great testimony to my parents that somehow, despite the futility of dad's attempt to leave us a sizeable patch of the perfect egg hiding turf, we managed to have a great Easter after all.

Getting Peeled

As a young boy, hardly any task was as dreaded as the "home grown" haircut. My dad had apparently learned how to cut hair while sitting in the barber's chair upon joining the Navy—at least he used the same boot camp techniques. Grabbing his equipment, he would march me off to the basement, like some middle ages executioner casting terror on his victim by showing off his instruments of torture before showing the victim to the castle dungeon.

Favoring the cement floor of the basement as prime haircutting territory, he would set me down in a blue vinyl chair from the kitchen table and wrap an old towel around my neck. Then, he would lovingly open a cardboard shoe box and pull out his old electric trimmers, a smooth, shiny masterpiece, its polished chrome form broken only by the black power switch and electric cord. Putting a few drops of oil in the shears, he would turn the unit with a loud vibrating hum, the suddenness of which always caused me to jump in the chair. As the shears began to purr, the smell of the light machine oil would permeate the air. Despite my father's assurances that the trimmers were safe, and that I could not be cut, I was convinced that one day he would slip and hollow out a major gouge in my scalp, or worse, lop off an entire ear.

Reaching again into the box, he would pull out several plastic adapters, designed to allow even novice barbers to cut different hair lengths expertly. Starting with a "tall" adapter, he would cut more and more hair in an attempt to get the perfect trim. Not satisfied with the results, he would move to progressively lower adapters, trying to obtain a uniform trim. Finally, in desperation he would give up and put on the lowest possible adapter and just skin my entire head to the point where even Kojak or Yul Brynner would have been proud.

My mother, who often stood nearby when I was subjected to my father's futile trimming iterations, would grumble at my dad in increasing degrees as the level of my hair grew shorter and shorter, until finally letting forth her patented "Ernie!" and marching back up the stairs, exaggerating her stomping footsteps to be sure her displeasure was properly registered. I can still remember crying during one of these sessions, begging him to leave me enough hair in the front to at least pass a comb through. If I were extremely fortunate, he would leave a small tuft of hair about one half of an inch long above my forehead.

As I grew older, my father fortunately "retired" his clippers and began taking me along with him to the "Modern" Barbershop on Pike street. This may have been a "modern" barbershop at one time, but was anything but that by the time my shadow crossed its well-worn doorframe. Nevertheless, I learned to love the environment of the old-time barbershop, with worn vinyl chairs, hair tonic and talcum powder smell, rotating barbershop pole, and archetypal barbershop barter. I still go to such an establishment today, spurning the more modern "salons" favored by my own boys. I have tried these shops, where women work over your hair with scissors instead of electric razors, but in the end I always go back to my roots, favoring having my hair cut by a licensed barber who will lather up my neck and sideburns to finish the job off with a straight razor. And, if he's in a good mood, he'll pull out his "electric massager" and work over my neck and shoulders, a treat you'll never get at a beauty salon.

A trip to the barbershop is fast, consistent, and reasonably priced. And, best of all, it is one of the last remaining bastions of manhood, the nearly secret domain of true men.

Doctor Jones

Today's pediatric doctor offices are designed to be appealing and kid-friendly. They are bright and open, with toys, games, magazines, and carpeted floors that appeal to young children. However, when Leslie and I were kids, the situation was regrettably much different.

Imagine the opposite of the warm, friendly office just described—that would be the office of our Doctor Jones. His office was on the second floor of a big, brown stone building in "town", which for us meant Parkersburg. Opening the side entrance door from street level, we walked up marble steps in the narrow stairwell, our footsteps echoing as we made the climb to the second floor. At the top, we passed through a mysterious door with a ceramic knob and a crystallized glass window at the top. Walking down yet another uncarpeted and windowless hallway, we finally opened the door leading into the waiting room. Our youthful imaginations worked overtime as we were pulled into this gloomy shop of trepidation.

If our anticipation of the examinations and shots were not enough, the dark dungeon decor made things even worse. Every sound, from doors closing to footsteps and crying children, echoed off of the bare walls and tiled floor. On many occasions we just gave in and just started crying before we even saw the doctor. We'd sit in the hard wooden chairs with white plastic padding, positioned all along the walls like silent sentries. Mom would tell the clerk we were there. Her only duty seemed to be keeping a stern eye on the assembled clientele, and the old woman was certainly a professional at her duties. It was a cold and scary atmosphere, and I was convinced that they were trying to scare us so bad that any punishment doled out by the doctor would seem a welcome relief.

The waiting room was always full of mothers and young children. Most of the kids looked very tired and sick, coughing and being cranky as we all waited in dread for our names to be called. Every click of the clock seemed like an eternity as we sat and silently pondered our bleak-looking future. This was boredom city; there were no toys, and the only real diversion was to walk over to the window, looking down at the street below.

Once our name was finally called, we would walk into his small office and anxiously wait for the doctor to come in, after sitting on the sterile and crackling white paper that covered the padded patient bench. Doctor Jones was an older man with snowy white hair, and he always wore a white lab coat over his dress clothes. He would step into the room, closing the heavy door behind him, jolting you to full attention. He would take his stethoscope and put the cold piece up against our chest or back and ask us to breathe in and out. This was a problem, as we were too scared to breathe, and the shock of the ice-cold stethoscope took our breath away. We were then poked, prodded, and every hole in our head was examined diligently for any sign of illness.

Inevitably, we had to get a shot. Even if we were in perfect health, he would flip through our records until gleefully finding that we were due for an immunization. Doctor Jones was apparently not a fan of oral medication, and it appeared that he graduated from medical school well before they had invented the pill. These were the days before disposable needles, so he would casually walk over to his Bunsen burner, where he sterilized his needles in a small pot of boiling water. The smell of alcohol and the fumes from the little blue flame captured our senses as we waited for the inevitable. Casually turning around, he kept one arm behind his back in a vain attempt to "hide" the needle. He would carefully take a cotton ball dipped in alcohol and would rub it in little circles on our arm (or some other part of the anatomy) and then get us to look "elsewhere" as he would jab the needle.

Doctor Jones also acted as his own nurse and bookkeeper. After our visit, he would announce the amount due, and it was paid in cash.

Taking the money, he would discretely slide it under the blotter on his desk, as if eager to do away with this unfriendly but necessary part of the visit.

We somehow survived these excursions, and were soon on our way with a big Band-Aid covering the sore spot on our arm. After making payment, we would make our way down all those big steps to the freedom of the outside world, having somehow survived another visit to the office of Doctor Jones.

The Happy Hollisters and the Bookmobile

During my late grade school years, I monitored the comings and goings of our mailman with great anticipation during the lazy summer months. Every day I would skip down to our large oversized metal mailbox, and was dutifully rewarded every two or three weeks in finding two books wrapped in cardboard. Ripping the cardboard off the precious payload, I would skip back up to the front porch, falling into the glider to begin immediately reading one of them before even taking the mail inside. It was not unusual for me to down one or even both of the hardcover books by the end of the day.

While J. K. Rowling captivates today's youth with her Harry Potter books, my generation grew up on Lassie, Tom Sawyer, and Huck Finn. I read over and over again classic stories like Treasure Island, The Swiss Family Robinson, and Moby Dick. For light reading, we would pick up copies of "Classics Illustrated", a sort of "Cliff's Notes" version of classic books in comic book format.

My favorites were the adventures of the "Happy Hollisters". This series of stories was about a family who somehow repeatedly found themselves in strange locations and ended up solving mysteries over and over again. It was sort of like a serious "Scooby Doo" without the talking dog and flower painted van. The titles of the books alone would make me salivate with anticipation—for example "The Swiss Echo Mystery", "The Sea Turtle Mystery", "The Happy Hollisters at Mystery Mountain" and "The Secret Fort." This was the neat stuff that tickled the imagination and let us wander far from the world we knew into a world of mystery and intrigue.

A few years later, my attention turned to Encyclopedia Brown and "60 second mysteries." I would pick up one of these every time the bookmobile came to Hopewell. As it ground to a stop in the gravel of the church parking lot, we would run barefoot through the cemetery and climb on board. The people who ran the bookmobile appeared glad to see anyone with an interest in reading, and did not mind how many books we checked out. For me, six books was light reading for two weeks, and I usually stocked up with eight or more. Arms loaded to maximum capacity, I would exit the bookmobile and head happily for home to begin a marathon session of reading.

My mother complained that this extreme amount of reading exacerbated the rate at which my glasses needed changing. Every year during my eye inspection, the mild-mannered Dr. Manzo would announce my need for yet stronger glasses, and every year my mother would ask the same question, "Does the amount of reading he does affect this?" And every year Dr. Manzo would give the same answer, not to worry, that reading a lot really didn't affect it much, and besides it was a good problem to have. Good for him anyway, as he sold us a new set of prescription lenses each year, plus did a good side business in all of the glasses that I broke while playing ball, rolling around, in bike crashes and the like. After a while my mother started keeping a box with all of the castaway frames, temples, lenses and screws, along with tape and super glue. She tried valiantly to mix and match temple pieces or front frames whenever I broke a set, working to keep my eyes open for business without the expensive trips to the city optometrist, in those days before we had Wal Mart and discount vision centers.

I had the privilege of doing most of my growing up before we had VCR's, video games and cable TV. Even to this day, my parents do not subscribe to cable, even though it finally made it to their part of the county a few years ago. Rather, we installed a large Radio Shack antenna, reaching above the rooftop to capture the invisible airwaves from the 3 or 4 local channels we could pick up. It was not unusual for us to set up a "chain of command", my dad trudging outside to turn the antenna, with two or three of us yelling "good!," "no, back a ways!," "there, that's it!" and similar pleadings until we got the channel we wanted to watch tuned to maximum effectiveness. My dad eventually wised up and installed an electric motor to allow "adjustment" of the antenna from inside the house, finally coming to his senses after we moved out of the house. I am convinced that he realized he could not hear my mom yelling adjustment instructions from the living room without intermediate parties carrying the message to the back side of the house.

We did have some music playing capability. My first experience was with an old Victrola my parents kept in the basement. It was actually functional, with a few old vinyl records like Eddie Albert's "Seven Years With the Wrong Woman." One year my sister Leslie and I got a small electric record player for Christmas, and we proceeded to stock up on a few albums and singles. In my time, I have passed through several "generations" of preferred musical media, from albums, to 8-track tapes, to cassette tapes, to CD's. (I just missed the "reel-to-reel" phase which hit it's peak before I was old enough to participate, thank goodness.) A few of my favorite albums have been purchased or "copied" on all four of these formats. Today, my children have only known the "CD" phase, and for their sake and my pocketbook's sake I hope the record companies keep with that format for a long time.

In the absence of the electronic babysitting and entertainment available today, my friends and I were forced to be more "creative", using our imagination to create toys and play situations. We would spend hour upon hour outside, building forts, making houses out of hay bales, and digging items out of the garage and barn to build carts, sleds, wooden guns, slingshots, and all sorts of playtime articles. Best of all, we voluntarily spent many hours reading, with no electronic distractions to draw us away from our books.

Although I enjoy a good movie as much as anyone, I am glad I had the opportunity to grow up without many media distractions. The absence of "pre-packaged" visual stimuli forced me to use my imagination, to hone my reading and writing abilities, and exercise my brain. I have no doubt I am better off for it today.

Games We Used to Play

My earliest "playtime" memory is of my beloved bear "Teddy." Teddy was my constant companion, and I would not go anywhere without him, especially to bed. Bedtime without Teddy was unthinkable, and my insistence on his nocturnal company caused much angst for my parents. Usually, this involved late-night searches through the house or yard for Teddy, trying to locate and retrieve him so I would finally get to sleep. My father grumbled under his voice as he trodded down the basement stairs, or headed outside with a flashlight to search the yard for my misplaced stuffed companion. On one occasion, I accidentally dropped Teddy in the toilet. Knowing I would require his company that night, my mother immediately set about throwing him in the old ringer washing machine, then she put him outside on the line to dry. There was Teddy, his bumpy fur freshly washed, drip-drying as he hung from the clothesline by his ears. I felt so sorry for him.

The games we played revealed our growing levels of maturity and exploration. As we got older, many of our playtime activities shifted to the basement. Here, in the wide-open space and concrete floor, we learned to roller skate. Our roller skates were quite crude, with metal "shoes" and metal wheels. They were worn over your shoes, and were a far cry from today's more technically advanced in-line Rollerblades and skates. Safety gear was non-existent in those days, and on several occasions we fell backwards, hitting our heads harshly on the concrete floor. We received several bad "bumps" and bruises, and were fortunate not to split our heads open.

During one hot summer day, we were playing barefoot in the basement, a good place to escape the summer heat and humidity. We had a small circular fan with had a metal frame. I reached over to move the fan, and when I grabbed the metal handle on top, the fan shorted and began electrocuting me. Due to the alternating AC current, I was unable to let go of the metal handle, and my hand gripped onto it tightly as 110 volts of electricity ran through my body. It seemed that time slowed down, as if the electricity somehow affected my brain waves. I remember Leslie yelling, and my own voice frozen in a silent scream, as I was unable to even call for help. Everything happened so clearly, like in a slow motion sequence, but I was only a spectator, unable to move. Finally, Leslie had the presence of mind to reach over and unplug the fan. It seemed like an eternity, but was probably over in ten seconds. I was lucky to have my older sister there with me, and we were fortunate that the fan had not shocked someone when they were alone in the basement. The results could have been disastrous.

When one of our friends got their hands on an old Ouiji board, we decided to hold a séance in our basement. This was the perfect location; private, dark, and close to the graveyard. We gathered some candles, creating the right mood, then set the board up on a table. Two of us grabbed the pointer, and after we settled down a little bit, things got more serious. We started asking for a spirit from the graveyard to speak to us. For a long time, nothing happened, but then the pointer started moving. I remember the name "John" being spelled out, along with a few brief and eerie phrases. We were really spooked, as we had not really expected anything to really happen. Finally, we grew so scared that we put the game up and never played with it again. For several days, we avoided the basement, and it took weeks to get over our sudden fear of playing near the graveyard at night.

Pigpen Follies

Given enough lazy summertime hours, and a lack of viable entertainment opportunities, a young boy will turn to just about anything to occupy the time. This was certainly true for me, as well as for my sisters, and any diversion or item that looked interesting served to engage our interest. Thus, we were more than happy to pass the time away by playing with the pigs in the pigpen.

Our pigpen was a strange looking structure, having been formed in phases using whatever construction materials were readily available to my father at the time. The entire pigpen had a wooden floor, keeping the pigs from "rooting" in the dirt underneath the wooden fence walls, which would have made short work of any fence. The front section, which was about the size of a small bedroom, was open to the sky and contained separate troughs for feeding and for water. Despite their reputation, pigs are actually clean animals, and the pigs we raised every year always took care to "do their business" (as we used to politely say) in the same corner of the pen, which made for easy cleaning. The back of the pigpen was covered with a roof, with a small door of about 3 foot square leading into the room, providing a dark and secure shelter for the swine. The ceiling of this room was low, about four feet off of the floor, and the floor was usually covered with a layer of hay for the pigs to lie in.

Along the sides of this structure, my father had built several rabbit cages, using the walls of the pigpen for the back edge of the hutches. Along with pigs and rabbits, the pigpen served as home for many other creatures, particularly under the wooden floor. Many an hour of my life was spent with long sticks, trying to chase out from under the pigpen small rabbits that had escaped from their cages. It was not unusual to see chipmunks, snakes, and other animals scurrying under the floor of the pen, and the roof was an ideal place for wasps and other insects. We spent many hours watching hornets flying low around the pigpen, and then swooping low to catch the flies that were feeding off of the pig waste.

We did not breed pigs, but only raised a few each year for slaughter. So every spring we would grab a gunnysack and head for Larry Townsend's farm to pick out a few piglets. After admiring the size of the huge sows in awe, we would pick out 2 or 3 piglets, usually from a litter of 10 or more. Then, throwing them into the sack, we tied the end shut with baler twine and threw the sack in the back of our truck for the ride home. It was quite comical, watching the sack ripple and swell as the piglets frantically moved around inside. Only by the grunting and squealing was it obvious what was inside.

Pigs will eat almost anything, and we made ample use of our table leftovers and garden to supplement their grain. The pigs accepted as delicacy rotten tomatoes, corn stalks, pumpkins, moldy bread, rotten milk and other items that we rejected. And although they never really were tame, we could still jump into the pen and play with them. My favorite pig activity was to grab a pig by the tail, then hold on for dear life as the pig tried to get away. Squealing in protest, the pigs would frantically pump their legs, but their heels would not get a good grip on the wet and slick wooden floor. Fortunately for them, a pig's tail is hard to hold on to, and after several seconds they would inevitably break free, scurrying off in their newfound freedom.

Our tendencies to play with the pigs caused major problems one year for my older sister, Leslie. She was just getting to the point where she still liked doing things like playing in the pigpen, but did not dare breathe word of this to any of her friends at school, who would have mocked her unmercifully if they knew where she wiled away her recreational hours. One fall, after the pigs had been slaughtered, we were playing in the pigpen, and Leslie turned to scamper into the inner room. Unfortunately, she did not duck low enough, and she hit her face on a board that formed part of an overhanging roof just over the door. Within a few hours, her eye turned blue, and she had a shiner that made it look like she had taken a punch straight to the eye.

Leslie was mortified. She knew she had to go to school the next day, but she dared not breathe a word to anyone that she had been playing in the family pigpen. The lobbying effort started immediately, and she tearfully begged all of us not to tell anyone how and where she had received her black eye.

This was, of course, not the first farmyard accident in the Dowler household. On one occasion, Leslie had climbed up a fencepost and jumped off, and a barb from the barbed-wire fence cut a deep and long gash into her leg, requiring many stitches. One of my first memories is hurting myself picking up a large rock, the end result being a minor hiatal hernia operation. I can still remember a foggy picture of the operation room at the hospital. On another occasion, I stuck a pitch-fork into my knee, and ended up getting tetanus. My knee got very stiff and locked up for a few days, until the medication relieved the symptoms. I was very fortunate not to break any bones as a child—to this day I have no idea how I escaped that fate. I always wanted to break a bone; it seemed so cool to have a cast, getting all of your friends to sign it. Then, my friend Darren Huffman broke both his arms at the same time while jumping off of a large propane tank, and he had to wear casts on both arms. For six weeks, his poor mother fed him, bathed him, dressed him, and did about everything else for him. That changed my mind on the allure of broken bones.

However, back to Leslie's dilemma. With the pigpen shiner, she was totally at our mercy. Like most younger brothers would be, I was dying to tell everyone what had happened. So she did the only thing she could do—she rallied mom and dad to her side. Before long, I was sworn to secrecy. We got by in telling a "half truth", that she had run into a "door frame" or something like that. Which was true, sort of. We just didn't say which door she had run into.

Eventually, my father quit raising pigs, and the pigpen fell into disrepair. Finally, we dismantled it, as it became an eyesore and haven for snakes, wasps, and other undesirable creatures. But, while it was in use, it served its purpose well. I would love to have some more of that homemade sausage, heavy on the sage and spices, lean and fresh, ground to the perfect consistency, fried in a skillet to a brown perfection and served up on a piece of my dad's buttered toast. Now that was breakfast.

My Life of Crime

I suppose every teenage boy gets involved in some sort of activity to push the envelope, to challenge authority, or take unreasonable risks in hopes of "getting away" with something he ought not be doing. Every now and then we pick up the paper and read about some young fool who has taken this nature to the extreme. But in most cases, as with my friends and I, we did things that were not worthy of the local news or a police line-up, thank goodness. In either case, better judgment gets clouded over by a combination of boredom, peer pressure, and testosterone, that mysterious chemical, which we had not yet learned how to properly handle in our formidable early teen years.

My life of crime started one winter Saturday morning, when I was hanging out with my friends Eric Bradley and Joey Phillips. Joey and I had sauntered over to the Bradley farm, supposedly to hang out, but primarily because Joey had a crush on Eric's younger sister. After getting bored of listening to Black Oak Arkansas albums, we decided to go outside for a walk in the snow. As if pulled by some force of gravity, we soon found ourselves perched on a cliff-like precipice, overlooking the cars driving some 30–40 feet below us on Route 68. The temptation was more than we could bear. As if each knew what the other was thinking, we reached down and began forming a small arsenal of snowballs.

Emboldened by the inaccessibility of our location, we began launching our frozen missiles at the unwitting drivers below. This required flinging the snowballs forward and at an upward angle, allowing the projectile to drift forward and downward in a 3–4 second free-fall until hitting the road below. At first, we missed the cars by a long shot, the snowballs taking much longer to fall than anticipated. With practice, however, we were able to improve our timing until finally one hit its mark, smashing down on the roof of a car with a loud thud. This went on for several minutes, with several cars falling victim to our bold barrage.

All was going well for us until about 15 minutes into our criminal activities, when a police car drove slowly up Route 68 and pulled off the side of the road next to our telltale snowball impact marks. We watched breathlessly in horror as he stepped out of his car, then turned to look up the steep embankment where we were crouched down, peering down through the brush in horror as our life flashed before our eyes. Fortunately for us, the policeman realized it would take him at least 15 minutes to climb up to where we were perched, and after pointing a long finger slowly in our direction, he jumped back in his car and drove up the hill. Sure he was going to come after us from another angle of attack, we abandoned our post and took off into the woods, racing as fast as we could go. You would have thought we were Cool Hand Luke, being pursued by bloodhounds and tireless state troopers with mirrored sunglasses and12 gauge shotguns.

Later that day, we finally worked up enough courage to leave the woods and run for our homes. The whole afternoon we were in agony, imagining that our parents would have been subjected to police interviews, just waiting for us to come home to get "what for." We were incredibly relieved to find out that our escapade was our own dirty little secret. We secretly thanked God and swore we would never do anything like that again. But not surprisingly, we were able to hold our criminal tendencies in check for only a few months.

In the late summer months, many apples begin falling off the trees, as if rejected by Mother Nature as unfit to grow onto maturity. Thus, the ground becomes littered with apples, most of which are golf-ball sized or slightly larger. These have to be picked up, or they attract yellow jackets by the hundreds, and squish into a mess under the wheels of the riding lawnmower. If they are really thick the mower can actually get hung up, sitting in one place, tires spinning with no friction on the slick, sticky mess. So usually we would pick them up and feed them to the rabbits or cows. But our favorite trick was to launch them into the atmosphere with sapling sticks.

A sapling stick is simply a long, flexible stick, usually a "feeder" limb growing up from the trunk of a maple tree. We would cut these sticks so that they were about six to eight feet long, with the diameter narrowing from about one inch at the base to one-half inch or less at the tip. At the tip we would sharpen the stick to a point, then push it into the green, fallen apples. Used properly, these sticks can be used to launch the apples the length of a football field or more.

There are two primary launching techniques; the straight-up and the roundabout. In the straight-up approach, you start with the apple on the tip of the rod, lying on the ground behind you. Lifting the rod forward by rotating your right arm, you swivel the apple over your right shoulder, launching it forward. In the roundabout method, you spin your entire body around, rotating the stick horizontally then stopping the rotation to whip the apple into the air. This gives great distance, but not much height, and is more difficult to control.

The secret to either method is how you start and stop the stick motion. Whip the stick too quickly at first, and it will accelerate away from the apple, leaving it lying on the ground at your feet. You have to start with a slow motion, building speed as you whip the sapling forward. To launch the apple, you have to suddenly stop the forward motion of the stick, causing the apple to disengage as the stick whips forward with maximum velocity. It sounds simple, but perfecting the technique requires hours of practice. Done properly, a small apple can be launched to impressive heights and distances.

One summer day, we decided to launch apples from the graveyard beside our house onto Route 68. This time Joey and Ronnie Breedlove were my accomplices in crime. We picked out three sticks, and each carried an armload of apples to our launching pad. Using gravestones for cover, we began launching apples toward the road. After getting the rhythm down, we could hit the road with fair consistency at best. We decided to start aiming for cars. This was tricky, as we had to start the process while the cars were still out of sight, and we had to judge our timing based on the sound of the vehicles approaching. The odds of hitting a car were so small, with the perfect timing required, that we were only doing it for the "rush" anyway.

This went on for some time, with several "close calls" but no direct hits. Then the improbable happened. I can still picture it today, as clear as if it just happened, playing out in slow motion before my very eyes. Hearing a pickup laboring down the road, I launched a large apple, about the size of a tennis ball, in a high, lazy arc toward the road. From its apex some 100 feet in the air, the apple fell to earth, picking up speed until landing with a surprisingly loud thud and splattering on the hood of the truck.

The poor guy must have thought his truck was falling apart, so loud was the impact of the apple on his hood. I'm sure he must have stopped to try to figure out what in the world happened, but we didn't stick around long enough to find out. Instead, we headed for cover, disappearing into the woods, leaving the apples and sticks behind as clear evidence of our foul play. Fortunately for us, the driver must have moved on, because a simple investigation would have easily revealed who was responsible. Once again, we escaped from our insurgence without punishment.

One Halloween night, we decided it would be fun to "corn" cars as they headed down Route 68. So we headed off to the tall grass in a field next to the road. Stripping handfuls of hard corn off of cobs, we would throw it, laughing as the corn made tink-tink sounds on the passing cars. This was real fun for us middle school pranksters, until one car screeched to a halt, and quickly made a turn, coming back toward us. Three large teenagers jumped out of the car with flashlights, starting back toward us in the darkness. We took off through the tall grass, taking different paths toward a getaway. The car looped back around us, coming off of the main highway to the dirt road behind us. Two more boys jumped out of the car, cutting off the escape path.

I soon realized I was surrounded. I had no recourse but to dive into the tall grass, hoping that somehow they would not see me. If I ran, my body would be exposed for them to see. The boys combed through the field, their flashlight beams passing over me as they moved around and past my position. I was sure I was in for a good beating if they found me. But by some miracle, they passed repeatedly around my hiding spot, but never saw me. After what seemed to be an eternity, as they began heading back to their car, I recognized one of the voices. It was my sister's boyfriend (and future husband) Dan Townsend. To this day I wonder if the fact that I was his girlfriend's brother would have saved me that night. I'm glad I never had to find out.

Bicycle Wars

The self-esteem of a young boy is often measured in terms of what he owns. It was no different among the lads of Hopewell Hill, and we were constantly comparing the slingshots, BB guns, footballs, and other items that we owned in hopes of outdoing and impressing our friends. This comparative self-worth was especially true when it came to our bicycles, for this was our primary means of transportation, and any perceived advantage led to instant jealousy among the other neighborhood kids.

This phenomenon did not occur all at once, but seemed to be a natural progression as we grew into our middle school years. Like most of my friends, early in life I had an old "junker" of a bicycle, a hand-me-down that my parents had likely obtained from some other family member or neighbor. The technology wars started slow. First, one of us would get a speedometer, allowing us to track our speed and distance traveled. Instantly, a chorus of whining could be heard for miles, as every other kid on Hopewell Hill began lobbying their parents for one also. After we all got speedometers, a steady-state condition would be met until one of us talked their parents into buying a generator and headlight for nighttime riding. And the vicious cycle would start all over again. Handlebar horns, spoke tubes, streamers, reflectors and name license plates were among the items we installed to set ourselves apart.

I felt I had finally one-upped this tit-for-tat rivalry, when my parents bought me a brand new 3-speed bicycle for my birthday. Not only was the bicycle new, but it also had a shifter, three glorious, individual gears, giving me an incredible edge at hill climbing and at top-end speeds. I was in my glory, and proudly rode my bike all over the neighborhood, just hoping that the kids in the neighborhood would see me riding and be jealous. My self-centered fame was short lived, as after only a few weeks my best friend Joey showed up riding a 10-speed. I did not even know that there was such as a thing as a ten-speed bicycle. I could see him getting a four speed, or maybe a five speed, but a ten-speed? And what was a derailleur anyway? That was totally unfair. And the handlebars! Who ever had seen such a funny system, with the pipes curved not outward, but under? The tires were so skinny that they seemed completely aerodynamic. Joey's bike was not just new, it was revolutionary. I was crushed. Not only was I outclassed, but with my bike being still brand new, there was no way out of my dilemma. I was forced into years of second-class citizenship with no immediate hope of rescue.

From time to time, we would be involved in wrecks, normally from sliding out on pebbles as we made a high speed turn on a gravel road. I had one wreck that was especially commemorative. Starting on Averill and Geneva's hill, we would ride down onto the old road in front of our house, often reaching speeds as high as 35 miles per hour, as measured on our speedometers. As we did this, we would often stand on the seat of our bikes or take our hands off of the handlebars, doing stunts for the audience of younger kids. On one such run, my bicycle oscillated out of control, and I plunged headlong off of the road, flying airborne smack into the middle of a large stand of briar bushes. I was deeply enmeshed in the bushes, and it took several minutes for me to gingerly pick my way out of the mess as the briars caught in my clothing and bit into my skin.

We initiated several spectacular wrecks as we attempted to navigate over "jumps" we created by propping lumber up at odd angles on a variety of blocks and stones. The worst such wreck occurred as our friend Wayne Townsend was visiting us one day. He charged down the road, hitting the ramp at an incredibly high rate of speed. I can still picture his wreck; the front end of his bike went high in the air, then as the momentum of his body kept moving forward, the nose dived downward, and he hit the ground with the rear tire almost straight above the front tire. His head and face plowed into the pavement, and he came up scraped and spitting blood. The rim of his front tire was bent, and his handlebars were twisted into a strange shape. Wayne was an instant hero, and he was immediately initiated into the Hopewell bicycle crash hall of fame. Our parents outlawed ramps from that point forward, and we were forced to move our extreme bicycle sports into more secluded areas.

During the summers, we routinely took daylong trips across the countryside. We would pack a lunch and a canteen of water, then head off down Pine Run or Gunners Run, branching off and exploring the country back roads that we rode for miles and miles. It was not unusual for us to get "lost", traveling into areas we had never been, and we would be forced to backtrack until we could find our way home. This was in the days before bicycle helmets were common, and I doubt we would have worn them even if we had them. Our parents did not worry much about our safety, as long as they knew we were to be home in time for dinner, and we heeded their admonitions to stay off of Route 68, which was called "the main road" by our parents.

Despite these admonitions, we enjoyed sneaking quick rides on the smooth blacktop, and would cruise at high speeds as the wind whipped through our hair. We were kings of our domain, ruling our neighborhood atop steeds of metal tubing. The world was ours as long as we had strength to pedal and an open road ahead of us.

Sledding

During the winter months, the youth of Hopewell Hill had limited entertainment opportunities. If we were lucky, our TV antennas picked up 3 or 4 channels at best, and this was in the days before home computers and video games had invaded our households. So, whenever we had snow on the ground, we headed for the hills and entertained ourselves with sledding.

Most of us had access to at least one store-bought runner sled, and we would polish and wax the runners in an effort to gain a slight edge over our neighbors. These sleds work best when you only have a few inches of snow on the ground, and they were the sleds of choice to go down dirt roads, where car tires had packed the snow into a hard icy surface. Pine Run was a prime spot, as we could start at the top of the hill, close to our house, and make a long run to the bottom. This often involved a "spotter", whose job was to yell a warning if a car was approaching around the blind curves of the road. After a while, this got boring, so we would spice things up by forming multiple-sled chains, or fashioning jumps or other hazards along the way.

During one Sunday afternoon, we discovered that these sleds had a serious down side. Taking a Sunday afternoon sledding excursion, we went down Pine Run to Earl Kaufman's farm. We picked a sloped part of the hillside, and began sledding. Jim Phillips, the minister at the Hopewell Church of Christ, decided to make a run with my best friend Joey on his back. At the bottom of the hill, there was a sudden transition from sloped to flat ground. When the sled hit this transition, the curved horizontal metal brace stuck into the ground, and Jim and Joey kept moving forward under the weight of their momentum. Most of that momentum was Jim's, as he is tall and was pretty solid in those days. Very little of the momentum was Joey's, as he was as thin as they come and would have blown off under the breeze going down the hill had he not clamped tightly onto his dad's backside. But Joey's body propelled forward, over his dad's head, and his weight was significant enough to prevent Jim from lifting his head as he slid forward. Jim's chin hit the metal bar at a high rate of speed, and split open like a ripe piece of fruit. Our laughter turned to blank stares as the dark red blood gushed out onto the white snow. After a trip to the emergency room and several stitches, Jim still got up on Sunday night to preach his sermon, true to the spirit of the tough West Virginia crowd who came to hear him out. Although he was not originally from the Hopewell area, the men of the congregation were proud of him nonetheless, and knew that they had hired a good man.

As a young teenager, I made my own sled, utilizing the workshop in the basement of our house. First, I made the short body of the sled, using rough-cut oak wooden boards. I then made two individual runner sections, one for the front of the sled, and one for the back. These were attached to the body of the sled using central pivot points—nothing fancy, just single bolts through holes drilled in the wood. The runner sections were connected using two sections of rope, which crossed over and formed and "X" shape. Thus, when I added a handle to the front section, and turned it to the right, the back section turned the same direction. This made it possible to slide sideways and traverse an incredibly tight turning radius. For runners, I split some one-inch plastic pipe, and nailed strips onto the bottom of the crude wooden runners. The end result was a heavy, crude sled that would move fast, turn very sharp corners, and consume high calories pulling it back up the hills. I was in poor man sledding heaven. I wish I had a picture of it.

Our favorite was deep snow sledding. It was not unusual for us to have 12 or more inches of snow on the ground at least once or twice during the winter season, and on occasion we could get much more. When the snow was really deep, we could actually make "toboggan runs" by shoveling out snow and forming a deep, curving depression down the hillside.

Sledding for us was more than a recreational activity; we took it seriously, and turned it into a science. Having limited funds, we often improvised, and anything that would slip and slide over snow was fair game. Among the items we routinely used were pieces of sheet metal, cardboard, plastic bags, car hoods, and my personal favorite, tractor tire inner tubes. These inner tubes were much larger than car tire tubes, and you could easily fit two or three kids on a single one. Barreling down the hill, the tube would rotate uncontrollably, and you just had to hang on for the ride.

Although we had many places where we could go sledding, our favorite place was on a hillside at Earl's farm. Here, a steep and broad pasture hillside sloped downward toward a small farm pond. On the hilly side of the pond, the bank ended several feet above the waterline, and we could fashion a jump that propelled us up and onto the frozen farm pond. Building up a head of steam, we would go flying, crashing down with a thud, sleds flying and arms and legs sprawling every direction, the ice creaking in protest under the impact. It's a miracle that we did not break through, drowning under the ice while contemplating our youthful stupidity.

Eulogies

I have been asked by several people to include copies of two eulogies in my book. These were written and read by me at the funerals of my father-in-law, Glenn Sadler, and my wife's uncle, Richard McKain. These two men died within a few months of each other in 2002.

I'll let the eulogies tell the stories of these two men. Although these eulogies are different from the bulk of my book, I feel they are appropriate, because they paint an image of two men who were typical of their generation. Their lives, values and influence are typical of the men who surrounded me in my own upbringing. This type of greatness should be remembered and reflected upon.

Glenn Sadler

Today Glenn's tired body finally lays to rest after a long and valiant struggle against a terrible illness.

But, if you would, imagine him running barefoot and carefree through the stubbled fields and bubbling streams of his boyhood home on Cherry Camp Road, the bottoms of his feet toughened by a long summer's activities. I can picture him tearing out of the freshly painted farmhouse, screen door slamming in his wake as he grabs a bamboo pole and can of worms and heads for the creek, yelling "I'll beat you" to his brother, their lean and tanned frames speeding into a competitive run. I see him swinging on a rope in the front yard, riding his bicycle on winding country roads, and learning to shoot a gun at his father's side. Growing up in the countryside, the appreciation of nature and the open outdoors was indelibly woven into the fabric of his being at a young age, as much a part of him as his own flesh and blood. His parents, who saw to it that a healthy dose of chores accompanied his carefree times on the farm, were carefully cultivating an appreciation of labor and a strong work ethic that would serve him well later in life.

Imagine Glenn as a teenage student, walking to his beloved Bristol High School on a crisp fall day. Despite the chill in the air, he leaves his jacket at home, preferring to endure the morning chill rather than be burdened by carrying it back in the warm afternoon. I can picture him in his khaki pants and a crisp, white shirt, leaning against the brick wall while hanging out with his friends, eagerly discussing the upcoming deer season or planning the weekend's events. The memories of his time at this small school were so strong, so burned into his memory, and so precious to him. Even after his mind was so ravaged by strokes that he could not recall his classmates names, he could open his fading yearbook and point at their pictures, telling you which ones in his class had died, who had moved away, the ones who had married, and other details of their lives.

After his junior year Glenn took a temporary break from school, joining the Navy as World War Two was drawing to a close. Like many of his friends, he answered the call to serve his country in a time when patriotism was strong, and the United States was coming to the rescue of the world. The military specialized in taking young men who had barely left the area of their childhood homes and sending them all over the world, and Glenn was no exception. I can picture him walking through the shipyard, duffel bag on his shoulder, looking wide-eyed up at the size of the floating steel city that he was about to join. It was on this ship, this mighty machine of war, that he sailed through seas as calm as glass, and through angry storms with 30-foot waves that tossed the giant vessel with indescribable power. Here the young country boy from West Virginia walked the streets of China and other exotic ports of call, with a proud swagger in his steps and muscles rippling beneath his dark blue uniform. He was proud of his service to his country, and loved to tell how he rode a train all the way across the country to return home after his two-year stint was over. And like steel hardened by working and fire, Glenn left the army with a tough, hard edge that he would keep most of his life, having served his country with honor and dignity.

Returning to finish his senior year, the calm and reserved Glenn was voted by his classmates to be the best dressed, and also to have the best hair. It was here that he noticed Norma Emerson, a junior who was attracted to his quiet confidence. Side-by-side, they endured the usual hardships of young married couples, including lean times, job searches, and even floods. Together, raising a family of three children, they formed a strong alliance, Norma the loving nurturer, and Glenn the strong provider.

Under the influence of his family, Glenn began attending church, and soon became baptized, showing them by his own life the importance of a relationship with Christ. Conquering his fears of public speaking, he even began presiding over the Lord's Supper. He took great pride in this service, and was sure to wear his suit and arrive 15 minutes early to church whenever called to serve.

During most of his adult life, Glenn was defined by his work at the Dupont Washington Works factory. Glenn was proud of his job, and it pleased him that he was able to work with his hands to support his family so well. Like most men of his generation, Glenn was a diligent and dependable worker, working around the clock, going for many of his years without taking sick days, and he seldom said no to requests to work overtime. Glenn and his co-workers took pride in their work ethic and the company that they served so well. As the country learned how to use the plastics invented in the great DuPont research laboratories, such as Nylon, Delrin, Teflon, Butacite and Acetyl, the company grew larger and stronger in the post-war expansion under the service of his grand generation.

At home, the neatness and order instilled by his military service served him well. In his prime, Glenn kept an immaculate shop. There was a place for every item. Every blade was sharp, every gear oiled, every motor well serviced. Glenn took great pride in the work of his hands. In his later years, he loved to reflect back on how he had built his shops and his garage, pouring all the concrete by hand, laying the bricks, running the wires, and framing the members in a toil of love until his dreams took shape. He took pride in his home, and worked hard to keep it in perfect condition. He would often use his carpentry skills for the benefit of others, whether building picnic tables for Ohio Valley College or lending a hand making bulletin boards, easels or bookcases for the North End Church of Christ.

It was only in his later years, when his mind began to decline, that we were blessed to see a side of Glenn that was new to us. It was if God, in his infinite wisdom, decided to temper the sting of his deterioration by softening Glenn's hard edge, giving us a tender, gentler image that we had never seen before. He began joking more, and enjoyed being around people more than in the past. He delighted us with practical jokes, hugs, and smiles. In his ailing condition, the first part of his mind to go seemed to be the years of proud bravado, the never-ending concern over appearance and formality, enabling him to easily say "I Love You" to his family for the first time. As layer after layer peeled away, we marveled at the inner beauty of this proud man, that we had never been invited to see during most of his life. As his decline deepened, the familiar phrases that he could still utter became fewer and fewer, until at last the only thing he could say was "The years go by faster…The years go by faster…"

Every life is a lesson, and Glenn lived his life in a way that we can all learn from:

- From his childhood, we learn the value of loving nature and God's creation.
- From his time in school, he taught us to cherish our friendships for a lifetime.
- From his military service, he taught us how to serve with honor and dignity.
- In his family life, he was an example of a strong provider who supplied for his family spiritually as well as physically.
- In his work, he was a pattern of dependable diligence that we should emulate.
- In his hobbies, he showed us the satisfaction and value of working with our hands to the benefit of others.
- And in his declining health, he showed us the value of inner beauty, and taught us to his last breath to value our time on earth, for the years really do go by fast.

Today, we ask that you remember Glenn, and take thought to how we can celebrate his years on this earth. By learning from his life, we can be inspired to live our own more fully and complete.

Jesus said, "I go to prepare a place for you. In my Father's house are many mansions..." I'm not sure what these spiritual mansions will be like, but in my imagination Glenn's mansion is not the largest on the block—that would not be important to him. But it is tidy and well maintained. When you get there, you'll find him in the back, in his immaculate workshop, strong and aware, taking great pleasure in putting the finishing touches on a labor of love that he meticulously prepared to welcome you on your arrival.

Dick McKain

If you would this morning, take a walk with me into the past, as we celebrate the life of this wonderful man, Dick McKain. His family would have you remember him from earlier times, as he lived his life in fullness and abundance. Dick and his twin brother Bob were the last of seven siblings, born in 1936 as the great depression was reluctantly loosening its grasp, being driven back into submission on the back-breaking work of great Americans like his parents, William and Millie. To fully understand Dick's life, you must know that he was born of tough stock. His father, appropriately nicknamed Slim, was a long-time military man and Seabee, who served this country in the Mexican conflict at the age of 15, and World War One, and World War Two, and went on to train troops for the Korean conflict as well. When he was not fighting in wars, he was delivering mail on his faithful mule, Jenny, on a tortuous 25-mile trek across mountainous dirt roads. On many winter days, his long legs would drag the snow, and he would stop at the blacksmith shop where they would literally chisel his feet out of the stirrups. Later, he bought a 1929 Jeep, which he modified by moving the springs above the axles to avoid getting hung up in deep muddy ruts.

As you look at the pictures of Dick as a child, you notice that he is always close to someone, whether his family, or his friends, usually touching them in some way. Tall for his age and slender, you can see that he was comfortable and relaxed with others, whether leaning with them against a car, hands in his pockets in a casual pose, or playing in the snow. In my imagination, I see him swinging on the porch swing of his single frame house, a pitcher of lemonade on the table next to him, reading a comic book in the lazy summer afternoon. Then, bounding down the stairs, he joins his brother and their friends, gripping worn baseball mitts under their arms as their high top canvas sneakers pound a path through the dirt streets of Wolf Summit, West Virginia. They stop periodically to check the status of their oiled and well-combed hair in car windows, then break into a proud swagger as they roll into the local field for their daily pick-up game.

As you look at pictures from just a few years ago, after some 50 years have passed, you can't help but notice similarities. You see that Dick is continually surrounded by family and friends, comfortable and relaxed, with smiles all around as they live their lives to the fullest together. As Dick grew, he was taught the value of hard work through chores, and in the example of his parent's lives. Like young Timothy in the Bible, Dick was unfailingly marched to church and taught by his mother and grandmother, with Bible stories and morality woven into the fabric of his consciousness at a young age at their unswerving hands.

Dick graduated in a class of 29 students at Bristol High School, a two-story brick structure on the hillside above Cherry Camp Road. It was here that this quiet young man met his future wife, Nola Emerson, though they did not start dating until after graduation. Dick was a very active student. He played baseball for three years, and was a pretty good pitcher. In the team photo, he stands in the back row, the tallest one on the team, and he used his lanky frame for leverage as he pitched for the Bisons. Dick was also on the yearbook staff, was football manager his junior year, was in the commercial club, and he sang in mixed chorus for 4 years. He was in the Thespians for two years, and was president of the Thespians and a member of the National Thespian Society his senior year.

Despite being turned down on his first request for a date, Dick was persistent, and he and Nola were married on December 15, 1956, in the Chestnut Street Church of Christ in Clarksburg. He started his career with the Crawley News Company, delivering papers and magazines. Then, following in his father's footsteps as a military man, he enlisted as a full-time company clerk in the National Guard. Like most men of his great generation, Dick was a dependable worker, rising early every morning, his uniform freshly starched and pressed, with creases down the sleeves and patent leather shoes polished to a brilliant shine. It was here that his patient and meticulous manner were of value, as he typed form after form on a manual typewriter. Loading the forms and carbon papers in the reel, each one had to be completed without a single mistake, as any error required starting over.

After a transfer to Parkersburg, Dick landed a job at Borg Warner Chemicals, compounding ABS plastics. The family has picture of him coming home after work, dressed sharply in dark pants and button-down shirt, with suede leather shoes, his metal lunch pail in tow at the end of his long, muscular arms. One of his son Mark's earliest memories is meeting his father after his shifts at work, running to grab that metal lunch bucket to see if there was a long stick of bubble gum waiting for him inside. As Dick's co-workers visited him in the hospital, without fail they would tell his family that Dick was a good example for everyone, honest, hard working, and a man of integrity.

As Mike and Mark grew older, Dick wisely decided that family time was more important than shift work differentials, and he took a pay cut to work a day job. This allowed him to do the things he loved the most, like playing with his boys, coaching their little league teams, and being present for each church service and activity. Among Mike's earliest memories of his father are the countless hours that they spent in the front yard, Mike pitching baseballs as his father coached him on throwing curve balls.

Dick loved spending time with Bud Emerson and Glenn Sadler, his brothers-in-law, and the three of them forged a friendship that was stronger than most brothers. These men fished, hunted, worked, camped, rode motorcycles, and raised their families together as they mellowed with age. If you don't know the Emerson family well, it is hard to truly understand their closeness. Dick was also an instrumental driver in planning the McKain family reunions, each one a massive undertaking, a true labor of love. Family was vital to him.

Several years ago, Dick's sister Kate gave him a Norman Rockwell cross-stitch, and he was hooked. Soon, he began buying Rockwell memorabilia, and as word spread, others began buying items for him as well. A walk in his home is like a tour of the Rockwell museum, with stamps, plates, ties, miniatures, puzzles, throw rugs, books, and even a Rockwell Bible. A highlight of his life was a visit to the Norman Rockwell home place in Stockridge Massachusetts. His favorite painting was "The Doctor and the Doll." I could not help but notice that the painting "Marriage License" was painted in 1955, one year before Dick and Nola were married. The works of Norman Rockwell connected with Dick on a deep level. His paintings embodied his values and morals, and reflected a simpler, idealistic time that he longed for and believed in. These works of art reflected an optimistic slice of Americana, showing the character of a people known well by Dick, who grew up in hard times and then passed through times of war, civil rights, boom times, the space age, and even today's marvels of computers and electronics. These works and their lessons of life permeated not just Dick's home, but also his life, demonstrating an optimistic celebration of what life can be.

Norman Rockwell once said, "*Some people have been kind enough to call me a fine artist. I've always called myself an illustrator. I'm not sure what the difference is. All I know is, whatever type of work I do, I try to give it my very best.*" Is it any wonder that Dick connected so intimately with the works of Rockwell? Like Rockwell, he gave his best in all that he did, whether in work, in love, or in service to others. Dick was truly an artist of life, and the people around him were the canvas on which he painted his works of devotion.

Dick made the most use of his time, whether traveling with Nola to see the country, or visiting his children, grandchildren, and friends. Dick fulfilled many of his lifelong dreams, such as attending a World Series, visiting an air traffic control tower, and hitting not just one, but two holes-in-one. He hit the second one on March 11 of this year, landing the double birdie with a 7-iron on the 4th hole of his beloved Worthington Golf Course.

Dick loved the game of golf. Until his recent illness, he would play almost every day, battling heat and cold, rain and sunshine. Like a good, meticulous military clerk, he kept track of every round, and every score, and was continually trying to improve upon his 83 average. He once calculated how many thousands of miles he had walked while playing golf—if only we could find that number! In his last days, as he slept under the influence of his pain killing medicines, he even played golf in his sleep, swinging a driver or making a key putt with his hands. On the courses, surrounded by trees, lakes, and rolling green grass, Dick felt a special closeness to God, as he relished the views and breathed in the smells of nature. He treated the game as he treated his life, each day a new challenge, making the most of every opportunity, testing himself, and enjoying the fellowship of his companions for each precious moment that God had given him.

Dick loved spending time with his grandchildren, and he referred to each of them with special nicknames he had created. Jobie was "Jober Jobes", Paige was "Tinky Tot", Ian was "Hammer Head", Meredith was "Snookems", and the twins were "Hannah Banana" and "Libby Lou." He worked hard to create special memories with each of them:

- Jobie remembers her grandfather's strong sense of family, how he would drive her half way to Ohio, so she was sure to spend time with her father.

- Paige was baptized by her grandfather. She remembers him for never getting mad or saying a cross word at any of his grandchildren. She loved when he would pick her up from school, then walk home with her, sharing in conversation.

- Ian was also baptized by his grandfather. Dick taught Ian how to play golf, and drove all the way to Wisconsin to be there for his "Grandparents Day" at school.

- Dick's influence on Meredith can be seen in her desire to buy "Pappy" a Popsicle every day that she visited him in the hospital, wanting to repay to him some of the kindness that he had shown her. Every night, as she would go to bed, she would bow her head and say in a soft voice, "God, Pappy's sick. Please bless Nana and Pappy. God bless Pappy's back, and God bless Pappy's lung. Just God bless Pappy."
- He hoped to someday take Hannah and Libby to National Twins Reunion. Unfortunately, he will never get to fulfill that dream.

As Dick became ill, his family rallied around him. As he came in and out of consciousness, he would greet each person in the room by name, and he kept up his spirit to the end. When he was moved to a private room, his roommate said, "I hate to see you go, because I know God will be going with you." In his life, Dick taught us how to live, and in his death, he taught us how to die.

"Jesus said, "I go to prepare a place for you. In my Father's house are many mansions…" Just a three months ago, I spoke at Glenn Sadler's funeral, and I said that while I'm not sure what these spiritual mansions will really be like, in my imagination I saw Glenn in the back of his tidy and well maintained home, in his immaculate workshop, strong and aware, taking great pleasure in putting the finishing touches on a labor of love that he was meticulously preparing to welcome someone else on their arrival. Today, we know who that first masterpiece was for. I imagine Glenn and many other brothers and sisters who have gone on before, greeting Dick, hugging each other, and walking into Heaven arm-in-arm. Only now there is a new aroma in Heaven, as Dick is in his kitchen, preparing tins of his patented peanut butter fudge. We look forward to seeing him there.

Afterword

Sir Winston Churchill once wrote, "*Writing a book is an adventure. To begin with, it is a toy and an amusement; then it becomes a mistress, and then it becomes a master, and then a tyrant. The last phase is that just as you are about to be reconciled to your servitude, you kill the monster, and fling him out to the public.*"

I must admit having felt the same way about this work. If it were not for all the words of encouragement by those with whom I shared my struggle, I would have given up a long time ago. I just hope that you found my little monster enjoyable.

About the Author

After completing a joy-filled childhood, Brian Dowler had a change of heart, and wisely decided to pursue engineering instead of journalism, completing a Master's Degree in Mechanical Engineering from West Virginia University in 1987. At the time of publication, Brian is the Director of Engineering for Graham Machinery Group of York, Pennsylvania. Brian resides in Camp Hill, Pennsylvania with his wife Cathy (Sadler) and children Ashley, Joshua and Jacob.

0-595-25880-8